THE SINGULAR FORTEAN SOCIETY'S

YULETIDE GUIDE *to* HIGH STRANGENESS

The Singular Fortean Society's Yuletide Guide to High Strangeness
Copyright ©2023 by Tobias Wayland, The Singular Fortean Society

ISBN: 9798867837426
First Edition

Cover, layout design, and illustrations by Emily Wayland
Foreword by Joshua Cutchin

PUBLISHING

*To our respective parents, Patrick and Cinda and Ron and Anne,
for always making the holidays magical.*

TABLE *of* CONTENTS

6 Foreword

8 Introduction

10 The Most Wonderful Time of the Year

12 The Devil's Pets

18 A Goatman By Any Other Name

24 It's a Cat's World

36 Everything Just Gets Weird

48 The Holidays Have Eyes

68 Along Comes Krampus

72 I'm Dreaming of a White Sheepsquatch

78 Long Nights

94 There Arose Such a Clatter

100 Wild Hunts

118 Santa's Little Helpers

124 Jolly Old St. Nicholas

132 Here Comes Santa Claus

159 Appendix A: The Mari Lwyd

163 Appendix B: Victorian Christmas Ghost Stories

FOREWORD

by Joshua Cutchin

Halloween gets all the love, doesn't it?

I mean, I completely understand why. I love it, too. The pageantry is all there—jack-o'-lanterns, witches, black cats, the whole nine yards—so people understandably get wrapped up in the spookiness of the whole affair. For a few brief weeks leading up to October 31st, Forteans of every stripe, from ghost hunters to cryptozoologists to ufologists, revel in the glory of our friends and neighbors being interested in the same things that we spend our lives thinking about.

And then (at least in America)… it's over, like an eclipsing moon slipping beyond totality. One day, people are willing to entertain our eccentricities; the next, we're back to being weirdos. Our interests fall out of alignment with the rest of the modern world, which moves on to the saccharine celebrations of an over-commercialized season we collectively refer to as "the holidays."

It's kind of a tragedy. Truth be told—if you live above the equator and are heading into winter—Halloween isn't the end of Spooky Season.

It's the *beginning*.

For centuries, many cultures in the northern hemisphere perceived the final three months of the calendar year as a long, slow slide into frigid darkness, only broken by the Winter Solstice and its redemptive promise of lengthening days. Until its arrival, the nights devoured more and more sunshine, providing ample shadows to cloak the unknown.

In Western Europe in particular, this creeping darkness was so influential that it spawned numerous traditions, beginning in mythology and folklore before culminating in the practice of Victorian "Christmas Ghost Stories" in England. Halloween is unquestionably the day of the year that you're most likely to run into goblins and ghouls… but a strong argument can be made that, historically speaking, Christmas is a close second.

For the most part, modern lifestyles have extinguished our awareness of that older darkness. Enter Tobias and Emily Wayland, who seek to rekindle it with *The Singular Fortean Society's Yuletide Guide to High Strangeness*.

When Tobias first mentioned this project to me in August of 2022, I felt two emotions: disappointment and relief. Disappointment, because the same topic was on my short list of possible future projects... and relief, because not only was there one less item on my "To-Do" list, but I also knew it was in incredibly capable hands.

That was more than a year ago. Today, I'm pleased to report that, through the use of the written word and illustrations, Tobias and Emily have succeeded in their mission to make the holiday season a little edgier, a little creepier, a little more magical, for the rest of us. This book confidently restores Christmastime to its rightful place in Spooky Season, where adults are allowed to share in a wonder solely reserved for children in our modern world.

Among its many approaches, *The Yuletide Guide to High Strangeness* links modern sightings back to old, sometimes even ancient, folkloric figures inextricably tied to the Christmas season. Alongside such deep connections, Tobias and Emily also mine the record for lovely, lesser-known gems that any Fortean might find surprising, including what may well prove to be a substantial contribution to the history of Wild Hunt sightings in North America. By the closing pages of this book, you will likely find Christmastime fully reenchanted, decades after you begrudgingly accepted the fact that Santa Claus isn't real.

Or is he? *The Singular Fortean Society's Yuletide Guide to High Strangeness* will have you reconsidering that position, if only slightly.

That's the wonderful thing about this book. In many respects, it does exactly what Christmas should—it cracks the calcified cynicism of adulthood, letting a little more wonder shine through.

After all, it's part of why we Forteans find the unexplained so compelling. We want to see through the eyes of a child, back to the age when we once thought anything possible, from ghosts to cryptids to elves—and, yes, even Santa Claus.

I'm sure you'll arrive at the same conclusion I did: the Waylands have managed to reignite that hope, like a bit of kindling piled on the dying Yule log of belief.

Introduction

It wasn't always so easy to forget our place in the world. Before many of us became disconnected from the food we eat and the land that provides it, there were natural cycles upon which we were much more dependent. Understanding those cycles could mean the difference between life and death, and certain times of year took on a special significance to our ancestors as a result—the echoes of which are still felt across modern culture.

Solstices and equinoxes were used to mark the corners of the year. They were how we knew when to plant and when to harvest, and of them, none embodied the duality of life and death quite like the winter solstice. Wintertime is a season fraught with endings—life and light temporarily leave the world to be replaced with a bleak stillness that itself was recognized as necessary for the spring fecundity to come. It's only natural that we celebrate this time of year, for both its cyclical role in nature and our own efforts to stave off the ever-creeping darkness that blankets the season.

The winter solstice took on a dark reputation in antiquity, and not just due to the lack of light. No, for many, this was a season for gathering relatives—living and deceased—and preparing to be visited by a variety of fantastical creatures, from elves to trolls to elder gods leading phantasmal hunts through dim forests. These things were very much on their minds as they thought of Yule, and even today, they're reflected in its remembrance.

Often, our ancestors were stuck inside with little to do during harsh winters and took to storytelling to stave off boredom. But that's not the only purpose served by telling stories. Stories can pass on knowledge, teach lessons, reinforce cultural ideals and taboos, or even act as a warning. Many of the subjects we will discuss in this book can be traced back to stories told during long European winters. The monsters we are about to meet will certainly fill some familiar folkloric roles, but there might be more to these stories than just staving off boredom or transferring cultural ideology.

These stories haven't stayed in our mythic past. They don't exist only in the cherished tradition of our annual retellings, but also in new experiences described by witnesses today, right now, in our world. There are still people claiming to have encountered fantastic beings, some of which mirror very closely the legendary figures passed down through time and memory. And that's enough for me to wonder why.

I'm willing to consider whether there might be an external cause to these experiences and the stories they so closely resemble. Perhaps we're not the only denizens of the planet who celebrate the winter solstice, or perhaps there are things out there which simply prefer the darkness that comes with it.

THE MOST WONDERFUL TIME OF THE YEAR

Before we begin, we had better have a brief discussion on the Germanic winter festival of Yule and what it is. What Yule isn't is the reason we celebrate Christmas on December 25th. That honor likely belongs to Saturnalia, a celebration of Saturn, the Roman god of agriculture, held every December. It involved a lot of feasting, gift-giving, and other merriment, and as Rome became increasingly Christian in the 4th century, the holiday was converted into Christmas to celebrate the birth of Jesus Christ instead of a pagan god. But Yule is responsible for many of the Christmastime figures and traditions we still hold dear today, as we'll see throughout this book.

As best we can tell, Yule may have originally been celebrated sometime in January, although modern adherents to traditional practices tend to center it around the winter solstice. This shift towards the solstice is likely due to its incorporation into Christian traditions during the conversion of Germanic peoples. King Haakon I of Norway, who ruled from 934 to 961, was the Christian leader of a largely heathen population credited in *The Saga of Hákon the Good* with passing a law stating Yule must be celebrated during the same time that Christians celebrated Christmas.

But more importantly than when it was practiced is what Yule represented. It was a time of sacrifice to the gods, and to venerate one's ancestors. Feasts were held and fires were lit to hold back the darkness and the things that dwelt within it. The Wild Hunt came during Yule, as did the unquiet dead—such as draugar—and it was not safe to wander alone at night.

We still hold so much of what Yule was in our hearts that we regularly refer to the Christmas season as Yuletide. Feasting and remembering our loved ones remain important parts of our winter celebrations, just as stories of Odin and his Wild Hunt helped shape our belief in Santa Claus. These stories and traditions are a part of us, for good or ill, and the question that burns in my mind now is: Did we create them, or did they create us?

THE DEVIL'S PETS

The Icelandic Yule Cat, or Jólakötturinn, is a creature known for its intolerance of laziness. This holiday horror was said to be a black cat as big as a house that used its height to look in the windows of Icelandic homesteads during Yule, hunting for those who had not received a gift of new clothing. New clothes were given as gifts to those hardworking Icelanders who had helped to process the fall's wool harvest prior to winter, and anyone whose clothing did not reflect the proper work ethic was taken and eaten by the Yule Cat.

The origin of the Yule Cat, like much of folklore, is difficult to pin down, but literary references to the creature can be traced back to the 19th century. Folklorist Jón Árnason wrote of the Yule Cat in his 1862 work, *Íslenzkar þjóðsögur og æfintýri,* "Icelandic Folk and Fairy Tales," where he referred to it as an "evil beast" that would either eat those who did not receive new clothing for Christmas or, at the very least, eat their jólarefur, a word used to describe holiday treats commonly given to folks on Christmas Eve.

Modern folklorist Árni Björnsson argued that the Yule Cat might not have been a monster at all, but rather, the idea that it was one arose out of a misinterpretation of the idiom "to dress the Yule Cat," which was sometimes said of people who had not received new clothes at Christmas. So, for instance, if you found yourself in that position, someone might say, "Looks like you've dressed the Yule cat!" Meaning, I suppose, that a cat must have received your clothes instead of you, and the word Yule was included only to signify the time of year, not to specify a singular monster that haunts the season.

Jólakötturinn/Yule Cat, illustration by Emily Wayland

Guðmundur Ólafsson, a senior researcher at the National Museum of Iceland and Björnsson's colleague, disagreed with his assessment, and pointed to commonalities between the Yule Cat and a creature sometimes said to accompany Saint Nicholas during the holidays: the Yule Goat.

The Yule Goat, or Julebukk in Norway and Julbock in Sweden, is best known today for its representation as a straw ornament tied with red ribbon, but its origin might lie in northern Europe's pagan past. One popular origin for the Yule Goat is that it was inspired by worship of the Norse god Thor, whose chariot was drawn by two goats, Tanngrisnir, "teeth bearer," and Tanngnjóstr, "teeth grinder." Another, potentially related, origin is that ancient peoples believed the last bundle of grain brought in each year contained the spirit of the harvest and thus saved it for their Yule celebration, referring to this bundle as the Yule Goat. Bundles of grain were sometimes referred to as goats due to the resemblance they bore to the animals. Notably, as mentioned in the *Prose Edda*, Thor was fond of cooking and eating his goats, only to resurrect them the next day, good as new.

In Sweden, as part of the Juleoffer, "Yule Sacrifice," a man dressed in goatskins and carrying an effigy of a goat head would be symbolically killed before returning to life, just as the sun returns after the winter solstice. Early Christian leaders rejected the pagan spectacle, declaring the Julbock to be a devil, and stories were told of how the caprine monster would roam the countryside, demanding food and terrifying the devout. Eventually, this tradition took on a more benevolent tone, with the Yule Goat becoming a helpful figure in Sweden, said to appear as an invisible ghost who observes households to ensure their holiday preparations are in order. From there, the holiday entity became known for its generosity, and merrymakers dressed as goats would travel door to door, distributing gifts.

In Norway and Denmark, the tradition was slightly different in a way that might be compared to a less offensive version of the early Christian stories, although it was said to still sometimes frighten children. There, people would go Julebukking, "Yule-Goating," by travelling from house to house, wearing masks and costumes, sometimes carrying a goat head fashioned from various materials on a stick, and singing carols in return for sweets and alcohol. These Julebukkers would attempt to disguise their voice, often by making animal noises or inhaling while speaking.

Another goat attached to winter festivities was the pre-Christian Slavic god Devac, who was depicted as a white goat. During Koliada—

Yule Goat, illustration by Emily Wayland

the Slavic term for the same period of the year as Yule—one celebrant would dress up as a goat and demand offerings in the form of presents. By the 11th century, this tradition had morphed into that of a man-sized goat led around by Saint Nicholas to symbolize his control over the Devil.

Ólafsson noted the relationship between goats and black cats—both popularly believed to be familiars in league with the Devil—and hypothesized that the Yule Cat may have begun as one of Saint Nicholas's followers. There is precious little historical evidence to support this, though, since so much has been lost to time. And even if we could trace the Yule Cat to Saint Nicholas, that wouldn't necessarily explain where the idea for it came from or why people felt it needed to be subjugated by the saint—only that it was associated with the Devil, which likely meant that they were afraid of it.

The strongest similarity between the Yule Cat and Yule Goat might be that there is no shortage of weird tales about anomalous cats and goatlike creatures, even today.

A GOATMAN BY ANY OTHER NAME

In both Texas and Wisconsin, there are legends of dead men sporting goatlike features who have come back to haunt lonely bridges and backroads.

Texas has Goatman's Bridge, near Denton, where the resident phantom is said to have the head of a goat.

In Wisconsin, rural Hogsback Road between Richfield and Erin is supposedly haunted by an apparition carrying the head of a goat, which he uses to scare drivers off the road's steep inclines to their death.

There are many such out-of-the-way places sharing eerily similar stories throughout the United States, although perhaps none are as well-known as Pope Lick Trestle Bridge in Louisville, Kentucky.

It's a popular location for monster hunting, and tales of the Pope Lick Monster date back decades. The monster is described most often as a human-goat hybrid, and according to some accounts, is said to lure passersby to their deaths—others say that he may be summoned by traversing the precarious trestle bridge.

Tragically, the bridge has been the site of several deaths and serious injuries since 2016.

In May of 2019, Savanna Bright, 15, was killed, and her friend Kaylee Keeling, 16, was critically injured after they were struck by a train while walking along Pope Lick Bridge.

Only three years prior to this tragedy, 26-year-old Ohio woman Roquel Bain was struck and killed while searching for the monster with her boyfriend.

Pope Lick Trestle Bridge, illustration by Emily Wayland

There are no official records documenting the total number of lives lost to the hunt for the legendary Goatman in Kentucky, but Louisville's *Courier Journal* published a 2016 interview with Wayne Gentry in which the retired train engineer said he had been involved in 43 collisions during his 34-year career with Norfolk Southern. Not every collision took place on the Pope Lick bridge, but Gentry did say that some of his fellow engineers refused to travel over the bridge because of the trauma involved in its frequent accidents.

Part of the bridge's inherent danger is that there is no way to avoid an oncoming train once someone has walked out onto the bridge. Platforms that had previously been placed along the bridge were taken down to deter pedestrians from walking along it. This lack of safety features combined with its older appearance providing the illusion that the tracks are no longer active makes the bridge exceedingly dangerous.

The safest thing about Pope Lick Trestle Bridge might actually be the Goatman, if there really is one.

Firsthand accounts of Goatman are exceedingly rare, even in the areas where they reputedly dwell (something easily attributed to the spread of urban legends), but not completely unheard of.

In 2014, author and Fortean researcher J. Nathan Couch published just such an account to his blog.

On October 28th of that year, a woman named Mindy Rossette posted to the Washington County Paranormal Facebook page about an encounter had by her and her daughter while driving near Holy Hill in Wisconsin.

"At the urging of friends, I am reaching out to you about an encounter me and my teen daughter had at about 9:40 p.m. on September 17th. We were traveling near Highway K and 167 near Holy Hill," she said. "I can only say [the creature] was maybe [four feet] tall, hairless, grey/brownish, and running on its hind legs. It seemed to brace for impact as my car barely missed it. […] Any ideas?"

Holy Hill, oddly enough, is located within a couple of miles of Hogsback Road.

"[The creature's] elbow was set low on the arm. Legs seemed to bend back at the knee like a dog's. Muscles very defined. Thighs especially. I couldn't make out the hands because of the way it was running. I couldn't

Goatman, illustration by Emily Wayland

see the feet as I couldn't see past the car hood," Rossette explained. "Instantly I knew this was something incredible. We were shocked and confused trying to figure out what the heck we just witnessed. We don't live far from that rural area, so we are pretty much freaked out to venture outside when it's pitch black. It's something we'll never forget. It was a monumental moment. The vision of this thing is etched in our lives."

Whatever it was, Rossette was certain that what they'd seen was real.

"I really want to know what that was. It was tangible. Not our imagination. I wish I'd seen the face, but it braced itself and tucked its head down. I wish I would have hit it. Not to cause harm, [but just so people won't think I'm crazy]," she added.

On February 20th, 2022, an anonymous user on the parental support website Mumsnet posted a report to the site's forum describing an early morning encounter with a mysterious creature on a road in rural England.

> We had been away for a few nights and travelled back quite late. Towards the end of our journey, this was about 2 a.m., we were driving along an A road in a rural area when something crossed the road in front of us in full headlights for about three seconds. It was about the height of a person, maybe six feet or over, but had short, powerful legs and hips which seemed to move in a circular, fluid fashion.
>
> It was not a deer, because it stood on two legs. This was in the Midlands and the area is traditional rolling fields and woodland. In this particular spot, there are no houses or buildings, nearest is over a mile away.
>
> We drove back today, as it's only seven miles from home, to look at the road layout, and whatever it was moved into a wide bowl-shaped field, dropping down to a stream. Any ideas?

The closest the witness could describe the creature, they said, "is [as] a large man-goat on hind legs, but really stocky ones."

They said the creature was "dark brown" in color, but that it is "always hard to tell in full beam."

The witness was travelling west on the A425, "after Staverton," when the sighting took place; near the border of Warwickshire and Northamptonshire, where the "road drops down a hill then rises back up again before the layby spot."

According to the witness's testimony, the creature "came from the gateway by the muckheap and crossed from [north] to [south] and into the field below."

The witness said they returned to investigate the next day, parking in the layby close to the sighting location, but there were no animals in the surrounding fields at that time.

Perhaps whatever these people encountered on the road those dark nights might have been called the Julbock or Devac had their sightings occurred in another time and place, and maybe, just maybe, the only thing that Hogsback Road's resident phantom is really guilty of is a little harmless Julebukking.

IT'S A CAT'S WORLD

There are no known species of big cats in Iceland that might explain the Yule Cat, although Icelanders do have a long history of strange cat-like creatures in their folklore.

The Skoffín, for instance, is said to be the hybrid offspring of a male arctic fox and female tabby cat. This creature reportedly resembles both parents, although precise descriptions vary; one thing that is consistent, though, is its short, patchy fur and the dreadful gaze that can kill anything the Skoffín looks at. And kill it does, being of a malevolent sort. Humans and livestock alike can find themselves unlucky victims of this monstrous amalgamation, although there are ways to fight back. The best strategy is to shoot them from a distance with a bullet made of either silver, hardened sheep dung, or a human knucklebone. Barring that, try to lure two of them together, since the Skoffín's gaze is deadly even against its own kind.

Similar to the Skoffín is the Skuggabaldur.

According to Árnason:

> A skuggabaldur has a cat for a father and a fox for a mother. They are no less a menace than foxes or other beasts that sorcerers send to kill the livestock of others. Guns are of no use against them.
>
> One time, a skuggabaldur who had done much harm to sheep in the county of Húnavatnssýsla was cornered in a hole and killed by a flock of men. As it was stabbed, the skuggabaldur uttered: "Tell the cat at Bollastaðir that skuggabaldur was stabbed today in the ravine." Those present found this highly peculiar.

Later that day, the man who killed the skuggabaldur came to Bollastaðir to stay the night there. That evening, he recounted the tale as he lay on his bed. An old tomcat sat on a crossbeam. But when the man recited the words spoken by the skuggabaldur, the cat leaped on him and fastened its claws and teeth into his neck. The cat could not be removed until its head had been cut off, but by then the man was dead.

Anomalous big cats are widely reported in other parts of the world, and perhaps nowhere has quite so many as the United Kingdom. Even within the last few years, I've reported on several sightings of anomalous big cats in the region.

If you're wondering how this relates to Iceland, well, I don't blame you. But consider this: trade between Iceland and various inhabitants of the UK goes back centuries, and where humans go, their stories are sure to follow.

On Saturday, May 27th, 2017, Emma Adam said she was walking with her mother-in-law at dusk along a woodland path near her home in Ashby, Northwest Leicestershire, England, when she spotted a large, anomalous black cat roaming her neighborhood.

According to Adam, the animal was eating something—possibly a rabbit or fox—and appeared malnourished.

"We were having a late barbecue, and I felt a bit bloated, so we decided to go for a walk," Adam said in an interview with *Burton Mail*.

It was getting late, so we decided to take a torch—there was just about enough light to walk. As we were coming along the path, I saw something lying down and I was trying to figure out what it was.

I kept looking at it, and I realized its head was going up and down because it was eating something, ripping it apart. My mother-in-law and I froze, and we just walked backwards. Luckily it didn't see us.

People were saying why didn't you take a picture of it, but in that moment, you are too frightened to take a picture. I always thought they would be very stocky, but this was much thinner.

I don't dare to go out on a walk, in case I see it again, I was looking at the laws to see what I can do to protect myself.

That was the second reported sighting in the area that year, after Phil Cross, a self-described wildlife "geek," said he saw a large black cat while on his way to a meeting. According to Cross, he witnessed what he described as a "black panther" blocking a countryside lane in Coton Park, just a few miles from Adam's sighting.

Three years later, a "large wildcat with big claws" was reported by an anonymous man to *Cambridgeshire Live* on April 11th, 2020, in Cambridge, England. Some speculated that perhaps the animal was related to the decades-old mystery of the 'Fen Tiger,' an anomalous big cat reportedly seen in the area since 1978.

The Fen Tiger is often described by witnesses as a large, dark, "puma-like" cat, as big or bigger than a Labrador dog.

According to the witness, this was not the first time he had seen the cat.

"It was around 8 or 8:30 a.m. this morning when I saw the animal from my kitchen window," the man said. "I think it somehow keeps coming to this place to hunt rabbits or other small animals."

"Initially I thought it was a wildcat like a *Felis Silvestris*, but then I went to my colleagues at the university, and they said it can't have been as this animal was way bigger," he continued. "Looking at the tail it's definitely a different species. It is a wild cat but not that species I don't think. The animal was a brown and black color with a very long tail that had lots of black circles on it. The tail was so long, and its legs were thick as well with big claws."

According to the witness, "it was about the size of a fully grown Labrador dog."

The *Felis Silvestris*, or European wildcat, is said to have been extirpated from England, although it is still indigenous to Scotland. They have irregular stripes, long, bushy tails, and male specimens can reach over two feet in length and weigh almost 20 pounds.

The man reportedly tried to contact local wildlife officials, but there was no immediate answer due to the coronavirus lockdown in his area.

"I rang the number but because of the pandemic everything has to be done through email, so I have sent one and I'm waiting for a reply," he said at the time.

Ultimately, the witness could not say for sure whether what he saw was related to stories of the Fen Tiger, but he did note some similarities.

"I have heard about the mystery of the Fen Tiger, but I don't know if this was it," he explained. "This was a wildcat like people have said the Fen Tiger is, and this one is the size of a Labrador dog."

That same year, two social media posts brought even more attention to the possibility of anomalous big cats in England.

The first was a report released anonymously through the private Facebook group Big Cats in Cumbria.

The witness explained that she noticed an unusually large feline when she stopped in the middle of the English countryside to get something out of her van. The exact location of the sighting was reportedly kept secret to prevent others from searching for the animal.

She said the cat was eating a pigeon as it watched her.

"At least one person had reported him crossing the road at night," the witness said. "I thought it was a lynx, but the markings are not there, and the tail is too long. I don't think he had tufted ears, but they had black tips."

According to Sharon Larkin-Snowden, listed as the Facebook group's administrator, "The witness said it was muscular and the size of a collie. Either a caracal or young puma. The size of the cat caught her attention [...] Maybe not our panther but this is one of the smaller big cats."

"She left it a chicken sandwich before she left after the sighting," Larkin-Snowden said. "She is going back just in case it's still about."

Opinions on what exactly the witness had seen varied, although common speculations included a young puma—also known as a panther, cougar, or mountain lion—a caracal, or a jungle cat. Pumas are big cats, native to the Americas, while both caracals and jungle cats are medium-sized wildcats native to parts of Africa and Asia.

Reports of big cats in Cumbria are relatively commonplace, with more than 40 sightings of a mysterious black panther reported since 2003, according to Cumbria Police. Although pumas are sometimes called panthers, the term black panther is generally applied to melanistic jaguars and leopards. True melanistic pumas do not officially exist, since so far none have been captured or killed.

The second sighting shared to social media came when an anonymous witness posted a warning to the Spotted Birstall Facebook page on April 29th, saying that their dog had been attacked by a "large cat" while they were "walking along the railway line towards the A46 Bridge."

> Walking today at 4 p.m. along the Railway track, I reached the A46 Bridge.
> My dog was ahead of me, and it turned right onto the small path after the bridge.
> I looked to my left and [saw] a large cat staring as I approached the bridge. It turned away, but my dog returned and [saw] the large cat and gave chase, stupidly.
> This cat stopped running and went for my dog, and they both bolted further into the wooded area. This cat would have got the better of my dog, and had I not been there screaming and shouting, I believe it would have killed my dog—which is a [112-pound] large dog. It's not exactly small, but this cat was bigger and longer. Please be on your guard for those that use this walkway.

Residents were quick to point out the area's history of big cat sightings, as well as share their own experiences.

"The comments about the big cat using the railways as its route to get about is correct," resident Amanda Berdinner said. "My daughter and I saw one, about 20 odd years ago, climbing in a tree to the side of the Great Central Railway track in Birstall (my garden backed onto the track). I remember ringing a gentleman who studied this for many years, which was reassuring as I honestly couldn't believe my eyes!"

"I remember looking at my tabby cat [sitting] on the kitchen table, then looking over towards the railway track and seeing what I'm sure was a black puma type big cat in a tree," she added. "It was using its large, low slung tail to balance which is exactly what big cats do!"

According to Victoria Louise, an employee with the Leicestershire County Council, "There has always been rumors of a puma that lives on the railway line, for as long as I can remember. I've never been lucky enough to see it, though."

Then, in December of 2021, an anonymous witness reported a seemingly large, dark-colored cat crossing a field in the Tynedale district of Northumberland, England.

According to *Chronicle Live*, the witness said they were working in the remote Allen Valleys when they spotted the creature from around 40 meters away, and that it "had to be bigger" than a normal cat.

Modern sightings of anomalous big cats in Tynedale date back at least two decades, with many witnesses having reportedly seen a large black panther in the area.

And on August 27th, 2023, a thirtysomething man who agreed only to the use of his first name, Jon, said that he had found a "half-eaten deer carcass" after spotting a big cat while walking with his family to Fernworthy Reservoir at Dartmoor in Devon, England.

"Whatever it was, my concern was that I didn't want it to come towards us. When I first saw it, I stopped straight away and told my family 'Don't panic and stay where you are. I think there's a big cat or dog up ahead," Jon told *Devon Live*. "It just felt a bit surreal and quite strange that my first thought was 'big cat'. [...] It had a huge tail, which must have been a meter long with some white on the end."

At first, Jon thought the animal was a stray dog, but after noting its features, he determined that it looked more like a big cat. Since he and his wife were with their son and one-year-old Labrador, they decided to turn around and walk instead to Grey Wethers stone circle. On their way, Jon said, they discovered a half-eaten deer carcass along the path, and later, when walking to their car, the family heard a disturbing roar.

We go walking on Dartmoor all the time and have done [so] for years. We were walking up one of the tracks with wife, son, and Labrador when quite far ahead I saw something which I assumed was a dog, but it looked massive.

It started walking around slowly then saw me, stood there and looked at me and then started casually walking away. I'm quite a calm character so I thought I was seeing things and remained calm as I had my dog and child with me and didn't want to panic them.

I thought I was seeing a massive dog, but my brain knew it wasn't as it was so bulky at the back end, the rear legs and back end were as bulky as the front end, and it looked very powerful and big. We decided to turn around as we had our one-year-old Labrador and our child with us.

We decided to walk back into the forest maybe a quarter of a mile further up and straight away my son said, 'what's that?'. There was a half-eaten deer carcass just off the path in the woods and in the path, there were quite a few bones about four to six inches long with broken bones from a rib cage.

We then had to walk through thick woodland to get back to the car and while we were walking, we heard a roar. We thought we were going mad.

But England isn't alone in hosting sightings of anomalous big cats.

In March of 2020, The Singular Fortean Society received an email from a man who claimed to have seen a large, black animal that "moved like a cat" in La Crosse, Wisconsin.

My friend and I were in the La Crosse River bottoms below Valley View Mall in La Crosse, [Wisconsin] yesterday. We saw the strangest thing. It was black and moved like a cat but [was] far too big to be a cat. The only thing I could even imagine was an otter. But I've seen many, many otters and it was too tall. But it was far too large to be a feral cat and totally black, so not a bobcat. My friend, who is not as into animals, had no doubt it was a cat by the way it moved. Very strange.

I scheduled a phone interview with the witness, but my call went unanswered, and I received no response to my attempts to reschedule.

Bobcats and mountain lions are the two largest species of cats most often found in Wisconsin, although according to the Wisconsin Department of Natural Resources (DNR), only bobcats are known to breed in the state. Adult mountain lions can be up to eight feet long with a 23-to-26-inch tail and weigh up to 160 pounds, standing 27 to 31 inches at the shoulder, while bobcats are around two-and-a-half feet long with five-to-nine-inch tails and weigh up to 40 pounds, standing 12 to 24 inches at the shoulder.

Melanism—the unusual development of dark color in the skin and fur—is not known to occur in mountain lions, but it has been seen in bobcats, regardless of the assertion made by the witness in his email. The condition is far from common in bobcats, however, and the only known specimens have been found in Florida and New Brunswick, Canada.

Sightings of anomalous big cats, often reported as being black, have been reported extensively around La Crosse and the area west of Baraboo, Wisconsin, as noted in *Return to Wildcat Mountain: Wisconsin's Black Panther Nexus,* a documentary by noted researcher, investigator, and author Linda Godfrey.

According to a description of the documentary provided by Godfrey,

> At first blush it seems a waste: a mountain lion's paradise, empty of lions for almost 100 years. But nestled among the rocky crags and lush valleys of this small area in west central Wisconsin, around 150 eyewitnesses say the big cats also known as pumas or cougars are returning—indeed, have already returned—to their old lairs and watered woodlands. Both tawny-colored animals and, surprisingly, black-furred big cats now strut these rolling hills. Area reporter Steve Stanek says the eyewitnesses are sure of what they've seen, but that according to science and wildlife experts, "black panthers" don't exist. The residents, who range from retired police officers to Amish farmers, beg to differ. The cats are back on Wildcat Mountain, they say, and this time, they show no signs of leaving.

Black Panther, illustration by Emily Wayland

Aleksandar Petakov's documentary, *Lions of the East*, makes a similar case for the decades of anomalous big cat sightings in New England — sightings that occur despite the U.S. Fish and Wildlife Service's claim that eastern mountain lions have been extinct since the 1930s.

The southern hemisphere also has its share of anomalous big cat sightings, as seen in these reports from New Zealand and Australia.

In May of 2019, Julieana Kavanagh was driving on the east coast of South Island, New Zealand, with her partner, Warren Lewis, when, at around 11:30 p.m., a huge, black animal bound across the road just a few feet in front of the car.

"It was in full flight; it was big and sleek and with a cat's head and a huge tail," Kavanagh told the *New Zealand Herald*. "We both looked at each other, thinking what the heck had just happened? We pulled off the road, slightly hysterical and went through every animal that it could possibly be, but nothing made sense. It was shocking."

The sighting came as Kavanagh slowed down to go around a bend in the road.

"It was just there, right in front of our headlights, right out of the blue," she said. "It was so quick; it was either chasing something or had heard our car."

But she was certain that what she saw was a black panther.

"A big cat isn't the first thing that we naturally thought of, after all we don't live in a country where you expect to see them. But that's what it was," Kavanagh said. "I don't scare easily, I've seen some shit, but it was big, quick and black and I was struck by how big its tail was. If that was a feral cat, it's a feral cat on steroids. Curiosity killed the cat but it's not the cat I'm worried about."

Kavanagh contacted the police and Ministry of Primary Industries about her encounter.

"I couldn't live with myself if I'd kept quiet and then it attacked a small child or livestock," she explained.

There are no known species of big cats that are native to New Zealand, but sightings of panthers have been reported on South Island since at least the 1990s; mostly centered around the Canterbury region.

Some believe the black panther sightings could come as a result of escapees from a private collection, although officials maintain they are simply misidentified feral cats.

In January of 2021, Australian man Michael Corr said he and his 11-year-old son were walking through the Tootgarook wetlands southeast of Melbourne on Victoria's Mornington Peninsula when they spotted an anomalous big cat.

"I just thought that's the biggest cat I've ever seen, and it was just crossing the tracks as if it was stalking something," Corr said. "My son ran in the other direction. We've been down there before and heard things rustling in the reeds but had never seen something like this."

After sharing his experience on social media, Corr said his inbox was "flooded" with messages from people who claimed to have seen black panthers in the same area. But many others who viewed the picture online were skeptical, dismissing it as either a large feral cat or a misidentified dog—possibly a black lab.

As for Corr, he said that the animal he saw definitely had the head of a cat and moved like a feline, and that there was no way he had misidentified a dog.

"I know feral cats get big, but it possibly could of been something else, as there are stories that go way back about panthers in the wild in Australia left from the travelling circus and also from World War Two," Corr said.

"My son is spinning out! He's doing research about [panthers], he's fascinated and a bit scared too," he added.

Controversy surrounding the existence of cryptid big cats in Australia has existed for over a century, with some believing that witnesses are misidentifying feral house cats, while others think the sightings could be explained by escaped exotic pets or even an undiscovered species of big cat native to Australia. The sightings are taken seriously enough that, in 2003, a New South Wales State Government inquiry found it "more likely than not" that a colony of "big cats" exists in the wilderness outside of Sydney. New South Wales borders Victoria to the north, and both states share a substantial amount of overlapping wilderness.

Repeatedly in various parts of the world, we've heard prosaic explanations for these anomalous big cats, from undiscovered animal species to escaped exotic pets, but perhaps we might consider something a little stranger. Something closer to the Skoffín and its ilk than any mundane animal.

Everything Just Gets Weird

In early January 2019, my friend Adam Benedict of the Pine Barrens Institute contacted me to share a report he had received two weeks prior from a woman who said she and her husband had seen a bizarre, chimeric creature in the spring of 2013 near Beloit, Wisconsin.

The couple's names have been withheld at their request.

In her initial email, the witness said that she and her husband had "just turned off Burton Street onto McKinley Avenue" and were "driving towards Newark Road" at approximately 4 p.m., when "across the field on the right [they] saw an animal by the tree line."

Her husband, who was driving, slowed down to get a better look at it, but traffic behind them forced the couple to keep driving. During their initial pass they saw an animal that "seemed to be on its back legs by a tree."

"It was barrel-shaped, and we were wondering if it was a bear. It dropped to all fours and started moving," the witness wrote. "We were debating if it was a bear, wild boar or the strangest dog we have ever seen."

Despite the witness' reservations that the animal would be gone if they went back, her husband decided to turn the car around for a second look. They drove back down McKinley, and performed a U-turn on Burton Street, which once again put the animal to their right. The pair pulled their car over onto the shoulder, and that's when, according to the witness, "everything just gets weird."

In a second email to Benedict the witness went into greater detail regarding the sighting.

> Up until this point I objectively believe my husband and I and the people in the car behind us saw a strange animal in the field. The rest of this story is my subjective experience. The animal was coming towards us. It moved like a cat, graceful with a long flicky tail. It didn't look like a cat though, except for the head. It was dark, but not black, brindled, dark browns with some black. The fur was short like a dog with some glossiness to it. Its head was massive, and triangle shaped, the eyes were large and green. The head looked so robust, like you could hit it with a bat, and it would break the bat. It was flat like a cat's, no snout like a dog or bear. Its chest was also triangle-shaped and really muscular with legs that came down like a bulldog's. The back end was a smaller triangle with legs that came off like a German Shepard. This thing was big and solid muscle. I think the top of its head would of came to my chin, so about four-foot. The tail was about the same length as the body.

The animal then began to amble towards them from about halfway across the field.

"This was what was confusing, it moved like a cat, but didn't look like one," she explained. "The whole time I had the feeling it knew we were watching and found the situation amusing. Also, the longer you watched it the harder it became to see it. Like its edges were blurring. It got to about 30 feet from the road and lied down, in a 'C' shape, just like a cat. It was staring at us, and I was staring at it. But the longer I looked at it, it almost seemed to become pixelated."

The couple then reportedly felt a sudden, overwhelming fear; something that has had a profound effect on how they chose to interpret the experience as individuals.

"I don't know how long this lasted, with a feeling of amusement on its side and wonder and confusion on our part," the witness said. "It changed in a heartbeat, the feeling that it could come through my window and bite my head off and my husband hitting the gas both seemed to happen at the same time."

"I looked at him and he goes, 'How was there no traffic?' It seemed like we had been parked for at least five minutes," she continued. "Then he said it was a dog. It was said in the tone of voice that says please let that of been a dog. If you ask him now, he will tell you we saw a deformed dog. I think he really needs it to be a dog, where I'm okay with living with not ever knowing. We were at the stop sign on Newark Road when it hit me that I was an idiot because I had my phone and could of taken a picture."

Soon after Adam shared the report with me, I was able to contact the witness and speak to her over the phone. She corroborated the details of her report with no embellishment and was consistent throughout the conversation.

"The more we tried to look at it the more confused we got," she explained. "It was laughing at us...it knew we were confused."

Towards the end of the encounter, the creature was only 20 to 30 feet from their vehicle, but they still were having trouble focusing on the details of its appearance.

"The edges of it were getting fuzzy. You couldn't focus on it," the witness said. "The harder you tried to look at it the less you were actually seeing."

And what their minds were able to comprehend simply didn't seem right.

"Everything about it was wrong," she said. "It was just like nothing fit."

The witness also said that the next day a friend and coworker confessed that she had experienced a similar event in the area.

"She's a hunter and she had no idea what she was looking at," the witness said of her friend's encounter. "That's the part that kind of bothers me the most."

When asked if perhaps the creature had been a ranging mountain lion, the witness was certain that it was not.

"I know what that kind of cat looks like," she said. "This thing was massive…a solid 300 lbs. Its head was triangular, and its eyes were far to the sides."

"I grew up in the country," she continued. "I've lived in this area my entire flipping life. The emotion was different [in this sighting]. We've seen stuff we couldn't immediately identify, but it didn't have this kind of 'through the looking glass' feeling."

Her sighting was followed by a similar encounter in August of 2019.

Emily and I were contacted by a man who said that he and his wife were driving home when they encountered a bizarre creature crossing the road just outside of Rockton, Illinois.

My wife and I were driving home the evening of August 8th, 2019. It was a little past 11 p.m. We were on South Bluff Road, heading north, having just turned off of Prairie Hill Road near the bridge. As we turned the corner, she first spotted "it" on the right side of the road, nearest the river.

She spotted eyes reflecting light, and assumed it was a normal animal (opossum or raccoon). I saw movement and said "deer", as whatever it was had longer front legs, like a tall dog. Then, as it crossed the road in front of us, we realized it was not a deer. Or any other easily recognized animal. I have grown up in rural areas and am well acquainted with various rural creatures. This was not a coyote or fox.

It had a rounded head and a flat face, no snout or muzzle. It had no obvious ears, or they were very tight against its head. Dark brown in color, almost muddy red in the car headlights. Long, slim tail that curled under as it loped across the road. It moved in a way that could only be compared to an ape or bear's style of movement, as if [moving on] all fours was faster but not completely necessary. My wife and I thought it moved like a gibbon. It left a bizarre impression on us both, as we can't settle on a creature that we believe it could be. The man described feeling a similar sense of high strangeness during his encounter as the woman with whom I had spoken earlier that year.

"There was definitely a sense of oddity, even now my head is trying to wriggle up a fit as to what it was. The whole incident lasted only a second or two," he said. "Amusingly, I live within five minutes of the first sighting."

He added that he had had some experiences with the unknown before the sighting, but none since—although his encounter with the phantom chimera did happen very recently.

"I actually have been quite interested in the grand 'Fortean unknown' for a long time. I've been part of a few 'haunt hunts', present at a seance or two. I've been to Bachelor's Grove, Gettysburg, and the grave of Inez Clark. Since [this sighting]? Not really. Been fairly quiet," he said.

He also shared a news article he had found from early July of 2019 in which a mountain lion was reportedly seen near Beloit by Orfordville resident Luke Reints. Interestingly, in the article, Reints never described a mountain lion; he said only that he had seen an animal resting underneath a bridge along the Rock River.

"I saw something out of the corner of my eye," he said. "It was kind of moving a little bit. I got the chills right away. I just started backing up all the way to my truck."

By the time Reints returned to the scene with a police officer, the animal was gone.

Those two reports led to another; this time out of Hartford, Wisconsin.

Christopher Pauls, 46, sent us an email on August 14th, 2023, with "Weird Animal Wisconsin" in the subject line.

> Came across your article about a strange animal sighting in Beloit, WI. I got excited when I read the description as it was exactly what I had seen many years earlier near Hartford, WI. I

was a kid when I saw it, but I often tell the story and when I read the witnesses' description of the animal to my wife she freaked out and told me I should tell someone my story.

During a phone interview, Christopher told me that his encounter had taken place during the afternoon of a sunny day sometime around mid-August between 1980 and 1982, when he was four or five years old.

His family lived at Saint Patrick Circle in Hartford, Wisconsin, at the time, and during the day he was watched by a babysitter only a few houses away.

On this particular afternoon, Christopher was being watched by his babysitter's 16-year-old son, Mike, while he rode his tricycle around a new cul-de-sac that had been built in the otherwise rural, isolated area.

"There was a big cornfield. That's what I remember," he said. "I was off in that circle area, just peddling away on my little tricycle and Mike had gone to the right, doing something, off doing his own thing."

At some point, he noticed that he and Mike were not alone.

"Just outside of the cornfield, there was like a 20- or 30-foot gap between the road and the cornfield where there was just grass. Right there, I see this big, black animal. It was just looking at me. It had been there longer than I had noticed it, because it was kind of fixed on me and then it started to like…I don't remember if it was ever still, but all I remember is seeing it trot next to me. So, not a stalking pose, but kind of an upright… it was like it was running next to me just to keep pace, sort of. I mean, not running, but trotting, I guess," Christopher said. "It was just fixed on me. It was staring right directly at me. It was about 10 feet from the cornfield, so maybe a third of the way towards the road. It must have only been 20 feet away from me. I was really close to it."

According to Christopher, the animal was quadrupedal and strongly resembled a big cat with a long tail.

"For a second, I thought it might be a mangey bear or something, but when I really thought about how it moved, I knew it was a cat," he said.

The creature stood approximately three feet high, and its body was three or four feet long. Its tail was roughly the length of its body, if not a little shorter.

"My first thought was that it looked like a black version of the Pink Panther cartoon. It had that jet black hair. It was skinny though. It moved like a cat, and it had a cat's tail. But the legs were longer for some reason. It wasn't that typical barrel [body] that you would see on a jaguar or a tiger, you know how they have that kind of wide midsection, and their legs are a little bit shorter. It was different from that," he explained. "And then the most unusual part was the head. One of the reasons that it did look like that cartoon is [its head] was really wide. It was very triangular in shape. I don't remember if the ears had any tufts or anything on there. It didn't have its mouth open, that's for sure. But I remember thinking that it looked like it was smiling. Completely black, but I think the eyes were yellow."

Oddest of all was the creature's face.

It was the face. The face was odd. It gave me that feeling like when you're spooked by something.

This was definitely one hundred percent an animal, but it had this almost human quality to it almost.

It was acting like it was either going to play with me or deciding whether to pursue me. It didn't make any noise or anything but just the look on its face was odd.

It may have been the smile feature, which I don't think was its mouth, I think it was some sort of marking or something.

I'm looking at it and my brain is trying to match up its face with something and it's not working.

Also strange, Christopher noted, was that he doesn't remember being afraid.

In total, the encounter lasted maybe 15 or 20 seconds.

"I tried to pedal faster," Christopher said. "I hadn't said anything or yelled out or anything, but Mike grabbed a stick, a big branch, and then kind of ran at it making a bunch of noise and chased it back into the cornfield."

Afterward, Christopher was left wondering what he had just witnessed.

"I asked [Mike] what it was, and he said, 'Oh, it was a wildcat,' and just kind of left it at that," Christopher said. "But I was going, 'That was not anything I have ever seen before.' I mean, I was young, but animals are like the first thing they show you. I had seen plenty of dogs, so I knew it couldn't have been a dog. I tried to ask his parents what that could have been, and they treated me like a kid. 'Don't worry about it,' they said. But it really kind of stuck with me because I had never seen anything like that. And I haven't seen anything like that since."

Decades later, Christopher saw something on television that grabbed his attention.

"It was when I was living in Boston," he said. "I was in a Dunkin' Donuts in Boston and I look up at a TV screen, it was like 2006, and it said that a DNR officer...something pulled a deer out of the back of his truck. It wasn't quite the description that I remember seeing, but I thought it was quite a coincidence. It kind of brought it back up in my mind. Made me wonder what in the hell that was. I know it was at Holy Hill, and that's very close to where I was living. I used to hang out at Holy Hill quite a bit, so I was like, 'Hey, I know that area.'"

The incident that Christopher referenced was originally reported by Steve Kreuger, a DNR contractor who was picking up animal carcasses near Holy Hill in November of 2006—only a few miles from the site of Christopher's encounter—when he said a strange creature, later dubbed a "Bearwolf," stole the body of a deer out of the bed of his truck.

While Christopher's experience doesn't exactly match that of Steve Kreuger, he also doesn't believe what he saw is easily explained as a mundane animal.

I'm an avid hiker, and I've had some experience volunteering with animals, checking trail cams and finding bobcats and cougars or whatever, and number one, for a cougar to come out of the woods by people where, you know, I definitely wasn't quiet, [is very unusual]. I mean, we had like 10 cougars in the state park that I used to work at, and no one saw one in like 12 years. They would just find the scat.

As far as appearance-wise, it could have been the same size as a cougar, but the face was not that of a cougar plus it was a little bit taller. First of all, the smile thing was weird, and it seemed to have a flat face. A cougar, to me, has [a more pronounced muzzle]. And the head on the cougar is typically a lot smaller than what I saw. This one had, like, this weird triangle-shaped head.

It was probably longer fur on its head, is what I'm thinking, and I know that lynxes can have this kind of mane almost. Some of them more than others and it depends on the season. It kind of looked like that, but it was bigger, I think, than a lynx or a bobcat. And a bobcat has those really long legs, but they're kind of hefty, their fur is kind of puffy. And I know it can kind of vary a bit, but this looked to me like it was a hybrid of like a cougar mated with a lynx or something and it just happened to be melanistic or whatever.

A lot of it had to do with the long legs as well. I mean, the face was really weird, but that could also be because it was black. I think that cats have a lot of markings on their face typically. It being all black probably made it look a lot scarier. And it didn't show dimension, you know. It was looking straight at me the whole time. I never caught a profile. But I remember it having a long tail, which kind of disqualifies a lynx or bobcat.

"It didn't look like any one animal that I've ever seen," he added.

Emily and I were also contacted through our website on February 27th, 2019, by a man who said he and a friend had seen a "shadowy man" transform into a "big, black, shadowy, cat-like creature" after suddenly appearing out of a "flash of bright light."

He asked to remain anonymous.

The following sounds crazy, but I promise it happened exactly as described. My wonder is if anyone has ever reported something similar. Years ago, a friend, myself, and my collie were sitting in my driveway around 11 p.m. just BSing on a summer night. Suddenly my dog began to go crazy and beg to go inside.

Then, across the street, there was a quick flash of bright

light and a shadowy man stepped out of the light.

The man turned to look at us, and as he/it did, it went down on all fours and went from a shadowy man to a big, black, shadowy, cat-like creature. There was another flash of light, and it was gone. During the event neither one of us spoke, but afterwards I looked at him and said, "do you want to go inside," he said, "yes," and so we did.

Inside, we took turns describing the event to each other and both of us saw the exact same thing. Years later, I ran into this friend again and he still remembers every detail exactly the same. No drugs or alcohol were involved nor had either of us tried any of that yet. It was clear as day and I remember every detail like it was yesterday. I know we saw something; I am wondering if anyone knows what it was.

After the witness initially contacted us, subsequent communication was done via email due to his schedule. He described a profound feeling of "nothingness" prior to the experience.

"It was very still, like described before a tornado hits," he said. "The only one affected prior to it appearing was my collie, Rocky. He went fucking nuts running from us to the side door, begging to go inside. Rocky was older and never acted that way. He would sometimes stay out all day or night just doing his thing. After it happens and we went in, that dog laid next to us or at our feet and never budged."

"A light breeze was blowing but had stopped prior to [the event]," he added. "No crickets, cicadas, when I say nothing, I mean NOTHING. It was as if everything else knew something was up."

According to him, this sighting took place in Richmond, Indiana, at around 11 p.m., in either the 3rd or 4th week of June 1993; he was not sure of the exact day.

Richmond is about 35 miles southeast of the Prairie Creek Reservoir, the site of a series of reports involving winged humanoids and glowing orbs. Indiana had seen a small flap of such reports a few years ago, not only near the reservoir, but also surrounding the city of Gary. The strange activity reported out of Gary, a city of over 75,000 that sits on the shore of Lake Michigan, included sightings of both winged humanoids and gigantic pterodactyls.

"As for other strange occurrences in the area, we had typical small, Midwestern town stories," the man said. "My friends and I used to go and look for supernatural occurrences. We had quite a few, but it was high school, and most could probably be chalked up to group hysterics."

But not the one he told me.

No, that experience stuck out as decidedly real, despite its impossibility. And we should consider what that might mean for all these phantom cats and the legends that have sprung up around them. If this man were to have witnessed the creature in just its big, black, shadowy, cat-like form, perhaps all we would have received is another anomalous big cat sighting.

Despite Björnsson's efforts to trace the origin of the Yule Cat to an idiom and the Yule Goat's various iterations, we must consider that, at one time, these might have been creatures that the people of Iceland and northern Europe treated very seriously, regardless of whether they were real in any physical sense. And the reason for that might have been as much because of some association with external phenomena as it was the various conflicting cultural influences that helped shape the stories surrounding them.

If there is something special about the winter solstice, then perhaps these stories were born in response to that. It's not unusual for folklore to be used as an explanation for something like a missing person, for instance, when no other explanation is forthcoming, and a giant, anthropophagus cat coupled with an obvious motivation might work as well as anything. The Yule Goat speaks to a more numinous reality, one populated with old gods and monsters venerated by a frightened populace to placate them as often as to seek favors. What the entities involved in those beliefs represent—whether cultural archetypes projected by humanity onto the universe or actual otherworldly beings of some kind—is unknown, but the impact is certainly felt, regardless.

For now, my advice is to pay proper respect to the annual harvest, and I hope your hard work has resulted in a gift of new clothing, because as we'll continue to see in later chapters, you never know what's lurking in the darkness, watching, this time of year.

THE HOLIDAYS
HAVE EYES

*All poems have been translated from Icelandic.

If you're wondering what kind of people might keep an enormous, man-eating cat as a pet, then allow me to introduce you to Grýla and her husband Leppalúði, along with their children, the Yule Lads. This cannibalistic family of trolls has been together for centuries, although the story of Grýla is older still.

The first mention of Grýla in literature is as one of several giantesses listed in Snorri Sturluson's Prose Edda, written in the early 13th century. This wasn't the limit of her popularity in that period and her name also appears in two contemporary historical sagas, Íslendinga saga and Sverris saga. And as Terry Gunnell, Professor of Folkloristics at the University of Iceland, pointed out in his contribution to the 2001 Nordic Yearbook of Folklore, Grýla may have been very popular indeed.

"With regard to Grýla, the number of extant thirteenth-century references stresses that the associations of her name must have been well-known to most people," he wrote. "No record, however, was ever made of what these associations were."

However, he continued, "Whatever Grýla was, there seems little question in Iceland at this time, her name was synonymous with something threatening."

There was even an early Icelandic expression that used her name, "að gera grýlu," which meant literally to "make a grýla," or in other words, to "show enmity."

By the 17th century, Grýla was being written about in more detail.

The poet Guðmundur Erlendsson described her as having horns like a goat, hair on her chin like knotted wool on a loom, a dirty mouth full of teeth, and wearing a shaggy, tattered skin coat.

Erlendsson, along with his contemporaries Stefán Ólafsson and Jón Samsonarson, wrote about how the hungry and animal-like Grýla would arrive at farmhouses, begging for children to eat, only to ultimately be rebuked, either having been given an offering to leave or forcibly driven away.

It was also during this time that she was connected to her family of fellow trolls and began to be associated with the holiday season.

In one of Erlendsson's poems, he writes:

Here's Grýla,
Peeking around a hill.
She will want to rest
Herself here all Christmas.

She will want to rest,
For here are children;
She is gray around the neck
And looks forward like an eagle.

She is gray around the neck
And runs down to the cowshed,
She does not want to look at
That festive light.

She does not want to hear
That festive song.
She complains of impotence
And claims to be hungry.

As the centuries passed, the Yule Lads became increasingly comic, although Grýla kept her edge, and her poor husband, Leppalúði, is hardly mentioned at all, unless it's to say how loathsome he is.

Grýla, illustration by Emily Wayland

One popular 19th-century verse from the Faroe Islands describes Grýla coming for children during Lent.

> Down comes Grýla from the outer fields.
> With forty tails.
> A bag on her back, a blade in her hand,
> Coming to carve out the stomachs of the children
> Who cry for meat during Lent.

In contrast to Grýla, the Yule Lads are more a benign set of tricksters said to come one by one and sneak into homesteads to spread mischief.

Beloved Icelandic poet Jóhannes úr Kötlum wrote of them in his 1932 poem Jólasveinarnir, which has defined how the Yule Lads have been seen ever since.

The thirteen Yule Lads, in the order they appear in Kötlum's poem, are:

- **Stekkjastaur,** "Sheep-Cote Clod," comes "stiff as wood, to pray upon the farmer's sheep as far as he could" because he "wished to suck the ewes." However, his stiff knees often prevent him from doing so.

- **Giljagaur,** "Gully Gawk," sneaks into cow barns and hides in the stalls to steal milk.

- **Stúfur,** "Stubby," is a "stunted little man" who is fond of stealing pans and eating any bits of food stuck to them.

- **Þvörusleikir,** "Spoon Licker," is as thin as a spindle and enjoys nothing more than stealing spoons used for stirring and licking them clean.

- **Pottaskefill,** "Pot Scraper," tricks children by knocking on the door, and when they rush to see if there is a guest, he hurries to the pot and has a "scraping fest."

- **Askasleikir,** "Bowl Licker," is "shockingly ill bred" and hides beneath children's beds, waiting for them to set a bowl on the floor to be licked clean by their dog or cat. When they do, he snatches it for himself.

- **Hurðaskellir,** "Door Slammer," waits until people go to sleep, at which time "he [is] happy as a lark with the havoc he could wreak, slamming doors and hearing the hinges on them squeak."

- **Skyrgámur,** "Skyr Gobbler," breaks the lid on skyr (a type of Icelandic yogurt) tubs and greedily gobbles everything within "until, about to burst, he would bleat, howl and groan."

- **Bjúgnakrækir,** "Sausage Swiper," steals sausages and absconds to a home's rafters before eating them.

- **Gluggagægir,** "Window Peeper," is a "weird little twit" who likes to look through people's windows and "whatever [is] inside to which his eye [is] drawn, he most likely [attempts] to take later on."

- **Gáttaþefur,** "Door Sniffer," is a "doltish lad and gross" who can catch "the scent of lace bread while leagues away still," presumably then following the smell right up to the door of the home producing it.

- **Ketkrókur,** "Meat Hook," arrives on Saint Thorlak's Day (the patron saint of Iceland) and uses his hook to snag any meat available.

- **Kertasníkir,** "Candle Beggar," follows children around to steal their tallow candles. Tallow, if you're not aware, is a rendered form of animal fat.

The prankish behavior ascribed to the Yule Lads isn't anything we haven't seen before. In faerie lore, a sufficiently angered Brownie might become a Boggart, this transformation leading to significant chaos in the household; stealing food, knocking things onto the floor, and generally disrupting the lives of those who upset him.

Stekkjastaur, illustration by Emily Wayland

Stekkjastaur, "Sheep-Cote Clod," comes "stiff as wood, to pray upon the farmer´s sheep as far as he could" because he "wished to suck the ewes." However, his stiff knees often prevent him from doing so.

Giljagaur, illustration by Emily Wayland

Giljagaur, "Gully Gawk," sneaks into cow barns and hides in the stalls to steal milk.

Stúfur, illustration by Emily Wayland

Stúfur, "Stubby," is a "stunted little man" who is fond of stealing pans and eating any bits of food stuck to them.

Þvörusleikir, illustration by Emily Wayland

Þvörusleikir, "Spoon Licker," is as thin as a spindle and enjoys nothing more than stealing spoons used for stirring and licking them clean.

Pottaskefill, illustration by Emily Wayland

Pottaskefill, "Pot Scraper," tricks children by knocking on the door, and when they rush to see if there is a guest, he hurries to the pot and has a "scraping fest."

Askasleikir, illustration by Emily Wayland

Askasleikir, "Bowl Licker," is "shockingly ill bred" and hides beneath children's beds, waiting for them to set a bowl on the floor to be licked clean by their dog or cat. When they do, he snatches it for himself.

Hurðaskellir, illustration by Emily Wayland

Hurðaskellir, "Door Slammer," waits until people go to sleep, at which time "he [is] happy as a lark with the havoc he could wreak, slamming doors and hearing the hinges on them squeak."

Skyrgámur, illustration by Emily Wayland

Skyrgámur, "Skyr Gobbler," breaks the lid on skyr (a type of Icelandic yogurt) tubs and greedily gobbles everything within "until, about to burst, he would bleat, howl and groan."

Bjúgnakrækir, illustration by Emily Wayland

Bjúgnakrækir, "Sausage Swiper," steals sausages and absconds to a home's rafters before eating them.

Gluggagægir, illustration by Emily Wayland

Gluggagægir, "Window Peeper," is a "weird little twit" who likes to look through people's windows and "whatever [is] inside to which his eye [is] drawn, he most likely [attempts] to take later on."

Gáttaþefur, illustration by Emily Wayland

Gáttaþefur, "Door Sniffer," is a "doltish lad and gross" who can catch "the scent of lace bread while leagues away still," presumably then following the smell right up to the door of the home producing it.

Ketkrókur, illustration by Emily Wayland

Ketkrókur, "Meat Hook," arrives on Saint Thorlak's Day (the patron saint of Iceland) and uses his hook to snag any meat available.

Kertasníkir, illustration by Emily Wayland

Kertasníkir, "Candle Beggar," follows children around to steal their tallow candles. Tallow, if you're not aware, is a rendered form of animal fat.

Similar, yet more terrifying, is the Bogie.

Bogies are malevolent faeries said to torture children who misbehave. Bogies often appear as shadowy, black humanoids, but sometimes take the shape of black dogs, tree trunks, or terrifying entities with icy fingers and glowing yellow eyes. Some stories of Bogies say that these frightening faeries will steal naughty children off to hell so the devil himself can torture them, although this is rarer than simply giving the youngsters a fright. Bogies can be found anywhere it is dark and dank; preferring cellars, attics, cupboards, closets, caves, hollow trees, or even under a misbehaving child's bed. Like Boggarts, Bogies will travel with offending families if they attempt to flee and moving to a new house is not a surefire method for ridding oneself of their presence.

Bogies are closely related to Bogles, who are frightening faeries said to perpetrate malicious pranks on much-deserving criminals and ne'er-do-wells. Unlike Bogies, Bogles rarely show themselves to their victims, but their presence can be felt by the overwhelming feeling of dread they evoke. When a Bogle does show himself, he appears as a dark, shadowy, thoroughly unpleasant figure; so much the better to terrorize those who have earned his wrath.

Very often different faeries appear practically identical, and only the activities in which they participate—which themselves are very similar—separate them, making it seem likely that they could be the same entity simply given a particular name depending on what they're doing; something which could be the case with Bogies and Bogles.

These similarities don't exclusively exist within categories of monsters or paranormal phenomena. The poltergeist phenomenon, for instance, shares many commonalities with the beings described above, including the disappearance of household items and a concerning focus on children. Fortunately, it's rare for that focus to translate into physical harm for the children involved, unlike what Grýla is said to do to them.

Grýla isn't alone in the danger she presents to children, either. To find a kindred soul to this cannibalistic troll, we need only look as far as Krampus.

Bogie, illustration by Emily Wayland

Along Comes
Krampus

The Germanic monster Krampus is most often depicted as a goat-legged devil covered in dark fur with long, curved horns. While his origin is a bit murky, some scholars believe Krampus to be a pre-Christian Alpine character.

Anthropologist John J. Honigmann wrote an article published in the Fall 1977 issue of *Ethos*, Journal of the Society for Psychological Anthropology, in which he described his visit to a Saint Nicholas festival in smalltown Austria that included Krampus, which he placed in the context of a "masked devil."

> The Saint Nicholas festival we are describing incorporates cultural elements widely distributed in Europe, in some cases going back to pre-Christian times. Nicholas himself became popular in Germany around the eleventh century. The feast dedicated to this patron of children is only one winter occasion in which children are the objects of special attention, others being Martinmas, the feast of the Holy Innocents, and New Year's Day. Masked devils acting boisterously and making nuisances of themselves are known in Germany since at least the sixteenth century while animal masked devils combining dreadful-comic (schauriglusting) antics appeared in Medieval church plays. [. . .]
>
> Austrians in the community we studied are quite aware of "heathen" elements being blended with Christian elements in the Saint Nicholas customs and in other traditional winter ceremonies. They believe Krampus derives from a pagan supernatural who was

Krampus, illustration by Emily Wayland

assimilated to the Christian devil.

As alluded to by Honigmann, Krampus is the antithesis of Saint Nicholas. Saint Nicholas, of course, is the popular figure given credit for much of the current mythology surrounding Santa Claus, although many of Santa's most notable aspects may actually come from pre-Christian beliefs, just like Krampus...but that's for another chapter. While Saint Nick brings presents to well-behaved boys and girls, Krampus beats bad children with birch sticks before throwing them into the basket he wears on his back and carrying them off to his lair in the underworld.

Like many preexisting pagan beliefs, Krampus was integrated into the Christian celebration of Christmas, although for years the Catholic Church attempted to suppress his inclusion as a form of demon worship. Despite the church's best efforts, celebrations involving Krampus made a resurgence at the end of the 20th century. Krampusnacht is traditionally held on December 5th, the evening prior to the Feast of Saint Nicholas, and features adults that dress as the demonic figure and parade through the streets—a tradition now held in a number of major cities across the western world.

Most interesting for our purposes are the similarities between Krampus, Grýla, and to a lesser extent, the Yule Lads. All three share an obsession with children, although there are few physical similarities between the hulking, hairy, horned Krampus and Grýla, and the diminutive and prankish Yule Lads. However, if we are in fact speculating about a range of phenomena that has a cause external to the human imagination, there might be an explanation for that.

In their book *Where the Footprints End, High Strangeness and the Bigfoot Phenomenon, Volume 1: Folklore*, authors Joshua Cutchin and Timothy Renner compare attributes of North America's most famous cryptid to anecdotes found in faerie lore.

According to the authors, "Faeries, however, were often shape or—more importantly—size shifters; one Scandinavian folktale relates a faerie changeling who stretched from infant-sized to as tall as a house, while a 1982 witness who encountered a 'Troll' in Minnesota—fat, stinking, in filthy overalls—alleged the creature grew eight inches and 50 pounds in a matter of seconds."

Something which could account for any size discrepancies we're likely to see, even in the house-sized Yule Cat.

Renner and Cutchin continue in their comparison, noting "Some researchers propose Trolls, along with Scottish Trows, were not faerie variants but instead misidentified bigfoot. Wrote author Njord Kane: 'If the North American bigfoot were seen a hundred years ago in Scandinavia, what would they call it? A Troll.' Harpur noted bigfoot, like Trolls, preferably inhabit 'vast, pretty much uninhabited, usually mountainous areas.' There is even a line of speculation that Grendel, antagonist of the Old English epic *Beowulf,* was based upon a bigfoot-like troll."

Our place here isn't to declare that Yuletide monsters are faeries or bigfoot or anything else, but rather to examine the similarities between them and other reported anomalies. And in the case of Krampus and Grýla, there is one very anomalous creature that immediately springs to mind. Their hirsute bodies and horned heads put me in mind of Sheepsquatch.

I'M DREAMING OF A WHITE SHEEPSQUATCH

A string of bizarre sightings across rural West Virginia in the mid-1990s birthed the legend of a beast that by all accounts appears to be an unnatural hybrid of sheep and Sasquatch. The often-unverified reports of these unusual encounters, which took place across Boone, Kanawha, Putnam, and Mason counties, describe a tall creature with shaggy white hair and long, ram-like horns—in other words, a Sheepsquatch.

Also known as the "White Thing," the earliest known sightings of this bizarre creature are said to have been reported in 1994, with perhaps the first of those being the tale told by a group of women driving near West Virginia's TNT area—a region already made famous among Forteans for its prevalence in the Point Pleasant Mothman sightings of 1966-67. This group of women were said to have been driving on an icy road near the TNT area when they were surprised by a large creature lumbering into their path out of the forest. The witnesses, who were moving appropriately slowly for the treacherous conditions, said they got a good look at the thing, which they described as being between seven and eight feet tall, covered with long, shaggy white hair, and a head with a pointed snout and ram-like horns. According to their story, the Sheepsquatch froze momentarily in their headlights before fleeing into the darkness.

Another well-known encounter to emerge from 1994 is that of former Navy seaman Edward Rollins, who was said to be out chasing Mothman reports along the bank of a creek north of Bethel Church Road in Mason County, when he was surprised by something large crashing through the brush in front of him. Thinking at first that it was likely a harmless member of the area's local fauna, he stood still to see what

Sheepsquatch, illustration by Emily Wayland

approached, hoping that he wasn't wrong. What he claimed to see was far stranger than he could have imagined; a large creature with dirty, matted white fur appeared within view of him and went to the creek.

It walked on all fours, but as it approached the water to drink, it did so with the help of forelimbs that ended in what looked more like hands than paws. The former seaman said the creature reeked of sulfur, although he thought that could be explained by his proximity to the TNT area, which is only a mile or two north of Bethel Church Road. The lingering pollutants from the manufacture of explosives had a sulfurous odor and were said to leech into the surrounding plants and animals. Rollins waited until the Sheepsquatch was finished drinking and had moved on before he felt comfortable enough to break cover and run back to the relative safety of his car.

Other reported accounts from that year include a motorist who said they witnessed a large creature with white fur on a hillside, and a group of children in Boone County who claimed to have seen a beast that looked like a white bear walking on its hind legs move along the edge of their property as they played outside in the yard—the beast allegedly fled at the sound of their screams, leaving a trail of snapped saplings and tree branches as evidence of its passing.

Sighting reports continued throughout the 1990s, including one story in 1995 of a couple being attacked by a white, bear-like creature while in their car. The couple had apparently slowed down while driving after spotting the beast in a roadside ditch. As they went by it, the being stood up on its hind legs, revealing a horned, four-eyed head that it used to bash the side of their car while simultaneously raking the vehicle with its claws. The terrified couple reportedly drove away at speed, only to find when they returned home that the side of their car was damaged by what looked like long claw marks.

Several years later, in 1999, a group of campers was supposedly scared off their campground by what they at first thought was a bear, only to be met by a huge, white monster lunging at them out of the forest. The beast gave an otherworldly scream, and the terrified campers fled for their lives—when they glanced back at their campground, they saw what they said was the Sheepsquatch staring them down from their former camp.

More recently, in 2013, an episode of Destination America's *Monsters and Mysteries* in America featured a 2004 encounter had by two hunters, Ricky Joyce and Dakota Cheeks. After the mysterious death of one of Joyce's dogs, the men said they were accosted by a large creature while staying in a camper near their hunting cabin. The thing shook and tore at their camper, but Joyce and Cheeks stayed perfectly still until it left. Once it did, the men grabbed their guns, stocked up on ammunition from the cabin, and tracked the creature through a cemetery to a field just beyond it. There, they reportedly saw a nine-foot-tall, white creature with long talons. The hunters shot at the beast after it growled and charged them, but either failed to hit it or it was unaffected by their firearms. Following the exchange, they fled back to the relative safety of their cabin.

That same episode featured the testimony of Susan Noe, a woman who said she'd seen a creature she described as "a big hairy thing standing on the road." Initially mistaking the creature for a deer, she soon realized it was far too big to be so easily explained and said instead that it was "some kind of sheep thing with horns."

And a 2014 episode of *Mountain Monsters*, also on Destination America, featured the testimony of two men who claimed to have encountered Sheepsquatch in Boone County. The first witness, Mason, said that he had come across a large, hairy creature while it ate from a deer feeder, and that said creature emitted a screeching growl and smelled musky. The second witness, David, said he was able to take a short video on his cell phone after seeing a large, brown, hairy creature attack a wood pile. A third man, Rocky, claimed to have captured a photograph of a large, mysterious, hairy creature on a trail cam, and said he found some of its scat when he went to investigate.

Finally, in 2015, a group of campers claim to have seen Sheepsquatch while camping in Fulks Run, Virginia. Their encounter began when one of them saw a strange creature crouching on a nearby hill around midnight. When he left to warn his fellows, the thing stood to its full height of between eight or nine feet tall and gave chase down the hill towards their camp. A river blocked the creature's path, and after failing to find a way around the obstruction the Sheepsquatch decided to wade into the water in pursuit. The curious campers gathered to watch the monster ford the river and said when it finally emerged that it resembled a large, white bipedal dog with long fur. Luckily, a shriek then emanated from the forest. This seemed to frighten the creature, which whimpered its way back into the woods, ending the encounter.

The narratives surrounding encounters with both Grýla and the Sheepsquatch share a certain similarity: creatures skulking around the edges of civilization, seeming to intrude only when fate or necessity require it. Much like Grýla—not to mention Krampus and the Yule Lads—

Sheepsquatch is a creature of rumor and legend. The sources of reports claiming sightings are often as difficult to track down as the origins of our Yuletide monsters. But there are enough people who publicly claimed to have encountered Sheepsquatch that I think it's fair to say at least some of them probably believe they've seen something very strange. Just as the people of Iceland and northern Europe might have experienced some otherworldly set of phenomena that inspired them to tell stories of cannibalistic trolls and cloven-hoofed kidnappers.

And who knows? Perhaps the inspirations for all these monsters are one and the same.

LONG

NIGHTS

During the Yuletide season it is said that the Anglo-Saxon god Woden, known more popularly by his Norse name, Odin, leads his Valkyries and einherjar—the souls of those who died in battle—astride spirit horses on a spectral hunt, late at night, accompanied by packs of vicious supernatural hounds. The souls of the dead are sometimes said to be carried on the winds of storms, and Woden is regarded as the god of both death and the sky, so it seems only appropriate that he be the one to lead these spirits in their pursuit. As Jacob Grimm noted in *Teutonic Mythology*, Woden is so connected to the phenomenon of howling wind in Scandinavia that it is sometimes referred to as "Odin's wagon." Furthermore, upon hearing a noise reminiscent of horses and carts at night in Sweden, one might remark "Oden far förbi" or "Odin fares nearby"; and in Germany, a nocturnal uproar heard in November or December is sometimes referred to as "Odens Jagd" or "Odin's hunt." The supernatural spectacle itself is known alternately as *Oskoreia*, "Terrifying Ride," or *Odensjakt*, "Odin's Hunt" in Scandinavia; *Wuotanes Her*, "Odin's Army," in Middle High German, and in Modern German as *wütende Heer*, "Furious Army," or *Wilde Jagd*, "Wild Hunt."

The demonization of pagan cultural remnants is something we've seen before and will continue to see throughout our examination of traditional beliefs. This association of pagan entities with demons and devils is a sort of connective tissue binding much of folklore together, and thus, we often need look no further than a story of the Devil to find an example of surviving pagan lore.

The Wild Hunt, illustration by Emily Wayland

Grimm wrote of post-pagan culture: "The Christians had not so quickly nor so completely renounced their faith in the gods of their fathers, that those imposing figures could all at once drop out of their memory. Obstinately clung to by some, they were merely assigned a new position more in the background. The former god lost his sociable character, his near familiar features, and assumed the aspect of a dark and dreadful power, that still had a certain amount of influence left. His hold lost upon men and their ministry, he wandered and hovered in the air, a spectre and a devil."

The incorporation of Christian mythology into the lore of the Wild Hunt is further evidenced by those iterations of the stories surrounding it which include the addition of any person who dies a violent death or unbaptized children among Woden's riders.

"As the Christian god has not made them his," Grimm wrote, "they fall due to the old heathen one."

This subsummation of the prior pagan culture sees Woden replaced entirely by the Devil in some stories, such as in Switzerland, where people tell of how the Devil leads a hunt on summer nights, cheering on his hounds, and riding over anyone unlucky enough to get in his way.

Another iteration of the Wild Huntsman is Hackelbärend, also known as Hackelbernd, Hackelberg, or Hackelblock.

According to Grimm, "Hackelbärend was a huntsman who went a hunting even on Sundays, for which desecration he was after death banished into the air, and there with his hound he must hunt night and day, and never rest. Some say, he only hunts in the twelve nights from Christmas to [Twelfth Day]; others, whenever the storm-wind howls, and therefore he is called by some the jol-jäger (Yule-hunter)."

Twelfth Day is an archaic term for Twelfth Night, which is a Christian festival that falls on either January 5th or 6th (depending on when you start counting) and marks the coming of Epiphany, a celebration held to commemorate the baptism of Jesus Christ and his manifestation in our world as the Son of God.

Grimm connects Hackelbärend to Woden by examining the name in its "most ancient and genuine" form of Hackelberend, which he then interprets to mean a man dressed in a cloak, based off the root word hökull, meaning "garment, cloak, cowl, [or] armour." Woden, or Odin, famously wore a broad-brimmed hat and blue cloak. Thus, Hackelbärend and his variations are, Grimm posits, "unmistakably an epithet of the heathen god Woden, which was gradually corrupted."

But it isn't only male figures attached to these wild hunts. In Germany, Switzerland, and Austria, there is Perchta—known alternatively as Berchta, Perahta, Berchte, Berhta, or Frau Perchta—who was also said to lead an ethereal army during Yule. She might appear as a wrinkled old hag with sharp eyes and a hooked nose, or as a beautiful young woman, although in either form she keeps her pure white hair.

Perchta is associated with the Germanic goddesses Frigg and Holda for her interest in the spinning of wool, domestic cleanliness, and children.

The last entry on that list is the saddest and most disturbing, since it is said to be dead children who accompany Perchta on her midnight marches.

Grimm wrote, "The little ones over whom she rules are human children who have died before baptism, and are thereby become her property. By these weeping babes is she surrounded..."

According to one tale about Perchta's procession of the dead:

> A young woman had lost her only child; she wept continually and could not be comforted. She ran out to the grave every night, and wailed so that the stones might have pitied her. The night before [Twelfth Day] she saw Perchta sweep past not far off; behind all the other children she noticed a little one with its shirt soaked quite through, carrying a jug of water in its hand, and so weary that it could not keep up with the rest; it stood still in trouble before a fence, over which Perchta strode and the children scrambled. At that moment the mother recognized her own child, came running up and lifted it over the fence. While she had it in her arms the child spoke, "Oh how warm a mother's hands are! But do not cry so much, else you cry my jug too full and heavy, see, I have already spilt it all over my shirt." From that night the mother ceased to weep.

Perchta's treatment of any girls or women who failed to meet her standards in the completion of their chores was almost as morbid, and arguably more gruesome.

It was expected by her that all weaving be done by Twelfth Day, that one's house be kept clean, and that a traditional bowl of porridge be left out as an offering.

And if these conditions were not met—the first two being more

Frau Perchta, illustration by Emily Wayland

important than the last—Perchta would disembowel the person responsible and stuff the empty cavity with rocks and straw.

Similar to Perchta is the creature known to Scandinavians as Lussi.

In Scandinavian tradition, December 13th was known as the longest night of the year, often referred to as Langnatt or "Long Night." Langnatt was ruled by Lussi, whose name translates to "light," and was said to be the time when she would lead a procession of faeries and the dead (two categories not easily separated) on her own Wild Hunt. The correlation between Lussi and light would continue even after the Christianization of her legend, when St. Lucia, who took over for the pagan character post conversion, would be most popularly depicted wearing a crown made of candles.

This night was considered dangerous. *In Keeping Christmas: Yuletide Traditions in Norway and the New Land*, author Kathleen Stokker wrote that tales surrounding Langnatt often dealt with "individuals being snatched up, carried away and then turned loose, dazed and manhandled, in some far-off place; other victims disappeared forever."

And just like Perchta, children had good reason to be especially fearful, since if they misbehaved, Lussi would come and snatch them, leading them up the chimney and away to the land of the dead. Also, like Perchta, Lussi demanded that all household chores be done prior to her night, although she paid special attention to cleaning, slaughtering, threshing, and the spinning of yarn.

People were understandably afraid to leave their homes on this night, and precautions were taken to ward off evil, such as the hanging of iron implements—like scissors, knives, and horseshoes—over their doorway. Iron, of course, has been used traditionally to repel faeries for centuries. Post conversion, Langnatt took on a more festive tone, and children would write Lussi on doors, walls, and fences to remind the malignant spirits of winter that their time grew short—since at that point she was associated with a Christian saint—and the bonfires lit were as much to celebrate the returning of the sun as to light one's way through the most dangerous night of the year.

But our purpose here is to concentrate on those things spoken of when the dark of night was still widely acknowledged to hold terrible things, not what we've told ourselves since to get through it.

Another Scandinavian tradition which tells of faeries moving throughout the land in great numbers during Yule is known as Asgardsreia,

St. Lucia, illustration by Emily Wayland

Lussi, illustration by Emily Wayland

or "Asgard's Ride."

During the Great Depression, the U.S. federal government created the Federal Writers' Project to provide jobs for out-of-work writers. As part of that project, a variety of folklore was recorded across the state of Wisconsin, including that of the "Hasgaardsreia"—an alternate spelling of Asgardsreia.

The name of the person interviewed close to a century ago has been lost to time, although the name Yudestad appears alongside Hasgaardreia in the entry title, referring to a farmhouse referenced in the story. United States Federal Census information from the early 20th century shows several residents with the last name Yudestad residing in Barron, Wisconsin, around the time the Federal Writers' Project was underway.

Barron, incidentally, is the site where, in 1919, 13-year-old Harry Anderson reportedly witnessed a faerie procession.

According to an article entitled *Encounters with Little Men*, written by Jerome Clark (under the pseudonym Alex Evans) in 1978 for Fate Magazine, young Harry was "driving with two friends and their father when their car ran out of oil and came to a stop east of Barron, Wisconsin."

Soon after, a local farmer who had been out fishing happened to walk by. When he heard what had happened, he offered to give the stranded motorists some oil, but only if one of them accompanied him to his house.

Harry agreed to retrieve the oil and walked two miles with the farmer back to his home. Afterward, he traveled back along the same one-track road.

The moon that night was full and bright, providing ample light for Harry to find his way...and much more besides. For there, in the moonlight, was a procession of little men.

Clark wrote that Harry witnessed "20 little men walking single file, heading toward him but paying no attention to him. Their heads were bald and the figures were dressed in leather 'knee-pants,' held up by suspenders over their shoulders. They wore no shirts and their skins were white. They were 'mumbling' but apparently not talking with one another."

Harry was "petrified with fear" and quickly continued on his way, not daring to look back.

And in a turn of events that we've seen far too often in the paranormal field, "When he got back to the car sometime later, he told his

Barron, Wisconsin Little Men Encounter, illustration by Emily Wayland

friends what he had seen. They laughed at him," Clark wrote.

After that, he told only his mother, and later, his wife. Both women believed that he had experienced something otherworldly.

I can't help but find it interesting to consider the synchronicity of this story potentially taking place in the same area of Wisconsin from whence came our tale of Asgardsreia (or Hasgaardsreia, depending on who's telling the story). Perhaps Barron, Wisconsin, really is home to little people who take to trooping across the landscape after dark, or perhaps these stories merely immigrated to the area along with the Scandinavians.

The following is taken from the testimony of our mysterious Wisconsin resident who spoke so freely of faerie processions back in the 1930s. The only unmarked edits I've made to the text are of spelling, punctuation, and paragraph breaks for ease of reading.

Hasgaardsreia is something peculiar to the Scandinavian countries—perhaps especially in Norway. On Christmas Eve the underground folk seem to get together in flocks, or considerable numbers, and go from place to place. And as they move about, they make much noise. Some describe them as hilarious and jolly; others say they indulge in howlings and screechings as they travel about. It is generally conceded that all kinds of fairies feel themselves under a certain ban—non-Christian and condemned to be shut out from heaven.

Learnedly and solemnly, through centuries, so-called Christians have discussed the status of fairies as to the question of final redemption and heavenly felicity. Perhaps most of our ancestors inclined to the belief that fairies will eventually be saved in a manner similar to so-called humans. And fairies perhaps join in this hope. But as centuries drift by and their status seems unchanged, they have become restless.

It is at Christmas that they express their dissatisfaction mostly. Therefore, on Christmas Eve, all decent and normal humans try to be at their homes early in the evening. But humans are subject to accidents, carelessness, and some to bad habits—such as drunkenness—and some do not reach home in seasonable time. If they are away, they are liable to encounter Hasgaardsreia on their way home.

A man in a community unavoidably on Christmas Eve,

was coming home late, when he met Hasgaardsreia. To prevent trouble, he lay down by the road, [and] stretched out his legs and arms. Lying thus supinely as the mob came by, one after another remarked, "There lies a cross." Fairies avoid crosses.

I never heard that Hasgaardsreia ever injured anyone severely — but usually those they encountered were badly harassed and half-scared to death and sometimes weak person were never quite right again after they had met Hasgaardsreia. Perhaps there is in Norway no superstition more common than the belief in Hasgaardsreia...

In conclusion, I will tell you a story about Hasgaardsreia.

In the days that are forgotten, in the unremembered ages, there lived in the parish where my mother was born a farmhouse known as Yudestad. Among all the farms in Norway, there is no more beautiful name than Yudestad in Bygstad parish. On this farm in the days that are forgotten lived a man with his wife and children. Legend tells us he was not a rich man — rather poor but comfortable and beautifully situated.

Except for one thing, he and his family might have been happy. But there was a shadow over his home which neither his ancestors nor he had been able to disperse. Like all good Christians he regarded Christmas as the sacrosanct holiday of the year — for this was the day when Christ was born to atone for the sins of the people who had lived on earth and all those still unborn.

Therefore, this family, living on Yudestad, had a right to rejoice, except for the fact that through many long years the occupants had to vacate their home on Christmas Eve, for every Christmas evening the Hasgaardseia claimed the use of this house for a feast. Wise men, good men, and holy men had been consulted, begged, and importuned to prevent or banish the underground people in the form of Hasgaardsreia, which affected this place. But to no effect.

Once more the glorious day was near. The family, in the falling shadows, was huddled in their primitive home getting ready to vacate the house when an old man suddenly opened the door and came in, bidding them the unusual courtesies of the occasion. As for instance, "God's peace be with this house and its folks. Happy Christmas and a good year." Indistinctly, the family mumbled from habit a kind of response. Then the old man, leaning one of his hands on a gun he carried, made this startling request, "I have come a long way, am very tired and hungry; please may I stay with you tonight?"

But for a moment neither wife nor husband made any reply. The old man, fearing his request was to be denied, continued, "I do not need to mention the sacred occasion of this hour in which I have met you, nor the many solemn injunctions which He, whose anniversary we are about to celebrate, has left behind for our instruction and salvation. He was all goodness, kindness, charity, and hospitality."

As he looked around, he found the wife and all the children were crying and the husband's eyes were misty with tears.

Then the husband spoke and said, "God help us, stranger! We are compelled to leave our home this evening. Therefore, we cannot entertain you."

Then he explained that he and his ancestors before him had for years been compelled to give up their home every Christmas Eve to Hasgaardsreia.

The old man listened to one of the strangest stories he had ever heard.

"But," he answered, "if you grant me permission to stay here, I will take my chances with Hasgaardsreia." This permission was granted, and the family left immediately. After they had gone, the old man looked about, laid off his outer garments and prepared for bed.

The house was of the common type, one single large room with a long table in the center of the room—probably twenty or twenty-four feet long. In one corner of the room a hearth built of rocks, perhaps seven feet or more high. This was called the "oven" in olden days. This so-called hearth or oven was used as a fireplace. As nearly as I can recall, it had an opening about three and a half feet wide, four and a half feet deep, and maybe five feet high.

At three o'clock p.m. during cold weather this space was filled with wood. When the wood had been reduced to coals, various kettles were suspended on cranes or supported on andirons where many kinds of food were prepared. I have forgotten to mention that this so-called fireplace had no chimney. Therefore, the smoke from the fireplace which naturally was produced all came out in front and filled the house. To get rid of the smoke, there was an opening in the center of the roof known as "Ljoren." When the smoke had cleared away, the "Ljoren" was covered by a trap-door in the roof.

From the trap-door hung a very substantial pole, the lower end reaching to about six feet above the floor. Old time houses had no ceilings. While the wood was burning, the front door was opened to permit escape of smoke. The fireplace was naturally built in by very substantial stones. The foundation may have been three to three and a half feet built up solidly from the floor. This foundation projected in front of the fire-box maybe two feet. This was the real hearth. Then over the fire-box were wide massive stones.

Therefore, on top of the fire-box or oven was a good place for sleeping—though rarely used for that purpose as it was too hot until late in the night. This oven, or fireplace, was very frequently called "Rauk-ovn"—"Rö-ovn." Those at fashionable houses were also very commonly called "Rauk-hus" or "Rög-hus."

It was on top of "Rauk-ovn" that the old man in this story elected to sleep. Here he lay down with his gun by his side to wait for what would happen. As Hasgaardsreia never move about until it is real night, the old man had a good rest before there were noises about the premises. Then he heard at first a murmur of voices in several keys, as if there were men, women, and children. But as the noises came nearer he heard laughter, hummings, and even songs. Then as the crowd neared the house there was a hubbub and babble of sounds increasing in intensity but rather like subdued excitement.

Old-time homes never were locked, so the latch was lifted and in a minute or two the room was filled to the limit. At first there was only a torch or two to light the room; in a few minutes there were more than a dozen torches and a lot of rush-lights carried by children.

One big fellow, who seemed to be a leader, circled the room while he seemed to sniff all about. Then he called loudly, "I smell Christian blood."

But several replied, "It's only a cat or Christian dog you smell."

This seemed to quiet all suspicion, and the women began at once to set the table. And when they had finished, the "Long Table" was loaded with such a variety of dishes and foods as the old man had never seen before during his long life. Dishes of gold, silver, crystals, carafes, beakers, goblets, chalices, decanters, cruses, bottles, and demijohns, all carved and ornamented. Many vessels were set with gold, silver, and jewels. Of foods there were too many to describe. On the floor and around on benches were casks, kegs, and even barrels, containing ales and liquors of various kinds.

As the old man watched the arrangement of seating the men and women around the table, he noticed they followed the customs usually observed by Christians. The more important and most richly and gaily dressed were seated first beginning at the head of the table and so on down to the end of the table. Most of them were richly appareled, with gold, silver, and beautiful gems.

At the head of the table sat a great big, fat fellow with three heads. After they had eaten for some time, a big man who sat on the right side of the three-headed monster rose and commanded attention. Then he raised a big goblet or beaker and said, "Now let us all 'skaal (a Scandinavian toast meaning "cheers") to—" I have forgotten the monster's name.

All the people with goblets in their hands rose, when suddenly from the top of the "Rauk-ovn" came a voice. "Yes, I have a skaal too, for the three-headed king of 'Yudestad Noset.'"

Then from the old man's gun sped a silver bullet which hit the monster squarely in the middle of his head. This caused the greatest haste and consternation while the banqueters fled from the house, where they left all their treasures, never to return to "Yudestad." From that time forth, the owners of the home lived in peace and great prosperity.

I have told this story as it was told to me by Mother and other neighbors while I was a boy. I am conscious of the fact that I have not told it as effectively as my mother told it first to me. One reason is that my mother told the story in greater detail and used many words and phrases I have forgotten. Besides, there are many idioms used in our country, which cannot be expressed in English. But you have the substance of a once popular tale in our community.

These tales of otherworldly home invasions and interrupted journeys remind me of a more modern intrusion into the lives of experiencers—alien abduction.

THERE AROSE SUCH A CLATTER

It was December 26th, 1985, the day after Christmas, when author Whitley Strieber had the experience that would drive him to investigate a series of strange events in his life and would ultimately lead him to write the book *Communion*.

Strieber was with his wife and son at their quiet, isolated cabin in upstate New York, celebrating the holiday season.

He had gone to bed that night after indulging a peculiar habit he said he had developed the previous fall, possibly linked to another incident with the strange visitors who would so profoundly impact his life. After putting his son to bed but before retiring for the evening, he would set the burglar alarm, which itself doesn't seem unusual, but then he would, as he wrote in *Communion*, make a "tour of the house, peering in closets and even looking under the guest-room bed for hidden intruders." Having completed the ritual, he and his wife then went to bed sometime before ten o'clock and were asleep by eleven.

So it was, then, on this cold and cloudy December night that Strieber awoke suddenly.

He insisted that, during the events to come, "I was not asleep, nor in a hypnopompic state between sleep and waking. I wish to be clear that I felt, at that moment, wide awake and in full possession of all my faculties."

It was the middle of the night and as he lay there in the dark, he heard a "peculiar whooshing, swirling noise coming from the living room downstairs."

Grey Alien, illustration by Emily Wayland

"This was no random creak, no settling of the house, but a sound as if a large number of people were moving rapidly around in the room," he wrote.

Sitting up in bed, Strieber struggled to understand what he was hearing. The night was calm with no wind and the burglar alarm remained armed. Whatever was making the noise, it wasn't the weather or some earthly intruder.

Despite the "edge of fear" to his shock and curiosity, he settled back into bed.

"For some reason the extreme strangeness of what I was feeling did not rouse me to action," Strieber explained.

As soon as he laid back down, he noticed movement at the bedroom door.

One of the outwards facing double doors leading into the room appeared to be moving closed, as though something from the outside was manipulating it.

At this point, he became "very uneasy" and once again sat up in bed.

It was then that Strieber saw a "compact figure" edging around the door and into their bedroom.

In the dim light provided by the glow of their home's burglar alarm combined with the ambient light reflected off the snow outside, he saw a figure "too small to be a person, unless a child," which stood at an estimated three and a half feet tall.

The figure was leaning around the door, exposing perhaps a third of its body.

"It had a smooth, rounded hat on, with an odd, sharp rim that jutted out easily four inches on the side I could see," Strieber wrote. "[...] From shoulder to midriff was the visible third of a square plate etched with concentric circles. This plate stretched from just below the chin to the waist area. [...] Beneath it was a rectangular appliance of the same type, which covered the lower waist to just above the knees."

Moments later, the strange being rushed into the bedroom.

Before blacking out, Strieber described how, when it was close to his bed, he saw "two dark holes for eyes and a black downturning line of a mouth that later became an O."

This encounter was merely the introduction to what would be a terrifying abduction experience for Strieber. One in which he would be taken from the cabin and flown to various locations to be examined by bizarre beings with indiscernible motives, not entirely unlike those throughout history who claim to have been accosted by faeries.

I recorded a similar account several years ago from a young woman in Janesville, Wisconsin, who wanted to report an encounter with "a grey thing with big black eyes" that occurred in her home during the spring of 2018.

The then 21-year-old woman had fallen asleep on the couch in her living room when she was awoken in the middle of the night by a bright light.

"I was woken up suddenly in the middle of the night from a very bright light shining through a small narrow window on the [front] door," she said.

The couch on which she had fallen asleep faces the front door, but the door itself is blocked from view by a wall. Anyone entering the home through the front door would need to turn immediately to their right and go around the wall to enter the living room.

"I had a roommate at the time, so I thought maybe it was her," the witness said. "As I stood up and slowly walked to the door, another thought came to my mind. What if it was a burglar?"

"I walked up to the door and suddenly, I was face to face with a grey thing with big black eyes standing there," she continued. "It honestly looked like your typical idea of what an alien would look like. It was slightly shorter than me, and I'm between 5'5" and 5'6"."

The witness screamed at the otherworldly intruder, and it shrieked back at her, its scream strange and birdlike.

"I screamed and it screamed back at me as if it didn't expect me to be there," she said. "I ran towards the kitchen and turned around towards my sister's bedroom."

It was then that she was struck by some sort of magnetic energy.

"It is very hard to describe," she explained. "Almost like electricity? Vibration? I was paralyzed. The entire room was lit up with that bright light and I was being pulled back to the couch."

She went on to describe the feeling caused by the energy as a "magnetic, tingling sensation," and said the light was bluish white in color.

Stuck in the magnetic energy's hold, the witness was pulled backwards towards the couch, her eyes closed in terror.

"I was floating," she said. "I was levitated above the couch I was originally sleeping in, and as soon as my body hit the couch, I 'woke up.' The living room was still as if nothing happened."

But the witness doesn't believe this was any dream.

"The entire time I was floating I told myself 'They're going to make you think this is a dream. They're going to make you think this didn't happen. It did happen. Don't forget," she emphasized.

She remembers her body bouncing off the couch as she was dropped unceremoniously onto it, and how she could feel its particular lumps press into her back as she landed. After she was returned to the couch, she opened her eyes to find that the living room "was still as if nothing happened."

The witness does not recall any gaps in memory or missing time during the event, nor did she find any out of place marks on her body afterward; although, admittedly, she did not specifically check for them.

Despite her surety she is still reluctant to discuss her experience.

"Everyone can just shrug it off as if it was just a dream," she said. "But I strongly feel that It was real. The fact that my initial reaction of someone coming inside was rational. The fact that I kept repeating to myself that this is real, it is happening, before I was brought back to the couch. It all seems and feels so real to me."

The witness explained that opening her eyes didn't feel like waking up in the traditional sense of a groggy return to awareness, but, rather, saying that she "woke up" was the best way to describe the return from paralysis, and she was otherwise continuously aware of her situation and surroundings.

"I think what I said is what happened," she added. "I truly believe it happened."

This young woman's experience implies a history of strange phenomena in her life, although this is the only conscious memory that she has of such an event. Certainly, for Strieber, his encounters with these frightening beings echoed forward and backward in time, proving to be a truly lifelong phenomenon for the author. In the same way, a pattern emerges out of these holiday stories. One that evidences a series of intrusions into human experience. These intrusions are not limited to home invasions, and it could be that warnings against travel during Yule are practical advice on some level, meant to keep our fellows safe from what has been interpreted by certain cultures as the Wild Hunt.

WILD

HUNTS

On December 26th, 1980, five years to the day before Strieber's abduction from his cabin, a series of strange lights were reported by military personnel stationed at Royal Air Force (RAF) Woodbridge in Suffolk, England. Because of the Cold War, RAF Woodbridge had been made available to the United States Air Force (USAF) and it was U.S. military personnel who witnessed the unusual phenomena. The lights were reportedly seen in Rendlesham Forest, located directly adjacent to the military base.

According to an unclassified memo from deputy base commander Lieutenant Colonel Charles J. Halt to the Ministry of Defence (MoD):

> 1. Early in the morning of [December 26h, 1980, at approximately 3 a.m.], two USAF security police patrolmen saw unusual lights outside the back gate at RAF Woodbridge. Thinking an aircraft might have crashed or been forced down, they called for permission to go outside the gate to investigate. The on-duty flight chief responded and allowed three patrolmen to proceed on foot. The individuals reported seeing a strange glowing object in the forest. The object was described as being metalic [sic] in appearance and triangular in shape, approximately two to three meters across the base and approximately two meters high. It illuminated the entire forest with a white light. The object itself has a pulsing red light on top and a bank(s) of blue lights underneath. The object was hovering or on legs. As the patrolmen approached the object, it maneuvered through the trees and disappeared. At this time the animals on a nearby farm went into a frenzy. The object was briefly sighted approximately an hour later near the

back gate.

2. The next day, three depressions [one and a half inches] deep and [seven inches] in diameter were found where the object had been sighted on the ground. The following night ([December 27th, 1980]) the area was checked for radiation. Beta/gamma readings of 0.1 milliroentgens were recorded with peak readings in the three depressions and near the center of the triangle formed by the depressions. A nearby tree had moderate (0.5 - 0.7) readings on the side of the tree toward the depressions.

3. Later in the night a red sun-like light was seen through the trees. It moved about and pulsed. At one point it appeared to throw off glowing particles and then broke into five separate white objects and then disappeared. Immediately thereafter, three star-like objects were noticed in the sky, two objects to the north and one to the south, all of which were about [10 degrees] off the horizon. The objects moved rapidly in sharp angular movements and displayed red, green and blue lights. The objects to the north appeared to be elliptical through an 8-12 power lens. They then turned to full circles. The objects to the north remained in the sky for an hour or more. The object to the south was visible for two or three hours and beamed down a stream of light from time to time. Numerous individuals, including the undersigned, witnessed the activities in paragraphs 2 and 3.

Charles J. Halt, Lt Col, USAF

Deputy Base Commander

The testimony of the men who went into the forest that first night varies, although they all agreed that they had seen anomalous lights. Some, like Airman Edward N. Cabansag and Airman First Class John Burroughs, would come to believe that a lighthouse was to blame, while others, like Staff-Sergeant Jim Penniston, were certain that what they'd seen was far stranger.

It's a contentious issue, and one on which much time and effort has been spent in service to both opposing viewpoints. While there are prosaic phenomena that could potentially explain the sighting, that's not the same as definitively doing so, and at this point, over 40 years later, we are left with little but conflicting testimony. Nothing short of a time machine is likely to solve this mystery, and so we must be content to accept it as unresolved. In this state, either opposing explanation could be true, and so it is not entirely inappropriate to consider either of them as such for the purpose of a phenomenological study of events.

Because of this, we will be treating the Rendlesham Forest incident as unexplained, with all the myriad possibilities that implies.

The men stationed at RAF Woodbridge aren't the only people to have seen weird lights around Christmastime. In January of 2022, I spoke with a man who said he had seen something very unusual indeed.

The Singular Fortean Society was contacted that month by Shane Taylor, 44, who wished to report an encounter with a multitude of seemingly friendly orange orbs he'd had on Christmas Eve of 2014.

Shane was driving on Zion Church Road near Hickory, North Carolina, at approximately 8 p.m., when an orange ball of light crossed quickly in front of him.

"Out of the blue, I'm driving down the road and this orange ball of light whizzes across my windshield, like an inch away," he told me during our interview. "I'm doing 55 miles per hour just zooming down the road and this orange ball of light just whizzes right by me."

Shane pulled his vehicle over next to an empty field and exited, only to find roughly a dozen silent, luminescent orbs "the size of cantaloupes" grouped together floating nearby.

Some were floating at eye level, he said, while others were a little higher than that, but they were close enough where Shane thought that if he had reached out, he could have almost touched one.

"I get out of my car and look up and there's like a dozen of these orange balls of light. Some of them were like five feet away, ten feet away, but they're all right there just hanging out," he said.

Each light would grow brighter or dimmer seemingly at random, while some hovered and others moved gracefully through the air.

"It was like you knew they were alive because of the pattern of the lights; similar to a heartbeat but it wasn't a repetitive thing," Shane said. "[Their movements were] the most beautiful thing I'd ever seen, really graceful, like a butterfly. Very smooth. It seemed like they could have gone any speed they wanted."

As Shane examined the orbs, he noticed that their insides "looked almost like the guts inside of a lightbulb."

"It's not light, it was some kind of structure," he explained.

Or so he thought.

"But right when I thought that it dimmed out where I could see it was light, there was no substance there," Shane said. "There was no structure; they would totally disappear and come right back."

He was at a total loss as to what the objects could be.

"I'm sitting there looking at these things, and, in my mind, I'm going through the rational things they could be. They're not lanterns, they're not drones, they were intelligent. Each one had its own personality almost," Shane said.

The awestruck man watched the orange orbs for several minutes, until they gathered together and left.

"The only time I noticed a pattern was when they left," he said. "They all flew into the same general area and flew away in a line. I watched them until they blinked out. They blinked out and there was nothing there."

Shane described the encounter as a strange, yet friendly, experience.

"It was really bizarre. There was a dreamlike quality to the experience, but I was still conscious and aware. It was really wild," he said. "When I got out of the car and they were right there it was almost like they were attracted to me; like they picked up on me and were like, 'Here's us, here's what we are.' To me it was friendly, like a friendly interaction. I know it's so weird to say interaction, but to me it felt that way."

When I asked him why he didn't attempt to record the experience,

Shane responded that it didn't feel right to try and do so at the time.

"I still didn't have a personal cellphone at that point. I had a work cellphone with a really crappy camera in it and I actually had my hand on it while this was going on and I swear it's the weirdest thing in the world, but I felt it would be rude. I didn't want to ruin the interaction," he said. "I remember thinking, 'I could try to get a picture but it's probably not going to come out good anyway, so I'm not even going to bother.'"

After the event, Shane noticed that a nearby church appeared to have ended its Christmas Eve service and the congregation was beginning to exit into the church's parking lot.

"After this happened, I was just standing there, shocked, and I could see over at the church, which was maybe a quarter mile away, I could see these people coming out of the church. There were maybe four or five of them," he said. "I was just so in awe that I left there and pulled into the church, and I asked these people, 'Did you see that?'"

The congregants' reactions to Shane's story were mixed.

"One guy was a real smartass and said, 'Yeah, it was Santa and his reindeer,' or something like that," Shane said. "But there was a woman in the group who was really interested. She asked me, 'What did they look like?' I still think about that. Why I did that. And I don't know, it was just such an intense experience. I wish I could have shared it with somebody."

It's possible that Shane did share the experience with other travelers that night, at least in some small way.

"Another funny thing, I was so focused on these lights, but I was aware that there were a couple cars that had gone by me on the side of the road with these things," he said. "And I thought in my head, 'How can you guys not see this?' I guess they didn't see it or if they saw it, they just kept driving."

The next day at Christmas, Shane woke up to his eyes almost swollen shut.

"My eyes were burning and red, and they were like that for two or three days," he said.

After that, Shane didn't think about the experience much for a few years, before deciding to investigate it further.

When he did, he discovered that there had been a major UFO flap on Christmas Eve and Christmas Day of 2014.

According to the National UFO Reporting Center (NUFORC), dozens of UFOs were reported on those two days, many of which bear an uncanny resemblance to the orange orbs described by Shane. From NUFORC:

One minute after midnight. Christmas Eve. Roseville, California:

Seven orange fireballs were reportedly seen.
The first three fireballs appeared in the shape of a triangle before "slowly burning across the sky" towards the north, followed by the remaining four which did the same.
The sighting lasted for roughly 45 seconds.

3:35 a.m. Christmas Eve. North Hollywood, California:

A witness said they had happened to look out of their kitchen window only to see a "large, very bright orange light, low in the sky, moving west to east."

"I immediately knew I was seeing something 'odd,'" they said. "So, I ran outside to get a better look."

Once outside, they said they saw an "extremely bright light" that was "orange in the center, and light orange and white on the very edge." They described the brightness of the object as "very intense." It made no sound.
The light was moving slowly and "made a slow/smooth move to the south" before the witness lost sight of it behind some trees.

This sighting also lasted 45 seconds.

6:45 p.m. Christmas Eve. Gilbert, Arizona:

Another witness was waiting at the intersection of Pecos Road and Higley Road when they saw three orange or amber lights.

"My husband asks, 'are those planes stacked up to land over there?', pointing to the [south/southwest], and we all start to look," they said. "He said there were three orange lights seeming to be in an arc — light planes lined up to come in as they turn — but these were holding still. He then said one seemed to dive down and swooped to the left and was abruptly gone. The second one started to fade out as two small [and fast] planes flew quickly towards them from the [southeast]."

When the reporting witness and their daughter looked, they both reportedly saw "one round amber light that was just sitting/floating in the air which then blinked out and disappeared."

"We are avid aviation fans who regularly go plane spotting, these were not planes nor were they   in the Phoenix Gateway or Mesa Gateway flight paths," they explained. "These lights had no beacons, and the color was between amber and orange."

In total, their sighting lasted about three minutes.

7:20 p.m. Christmas Eve. Pasadena, Maryland:

A witness reportedly saw "12 objects, with reddish orange lights, low in the cloudy sky."

"It started with two reddish orange lights, side by side, moving low across the cloudy night sky," they said in their report. "The objects were moving from southwest to northeast. They were well below the clouds, and they made no sounds."

As they stood watching the two lights, six more appeared behind them, flying in what the witness described as a Z formation. After those, two more appeared. All the lights were the same reddish orange.

The first 10 lights were seen from the front of their house, but when they went to their back deck, they spotted two more. Those two were a little farther to the north than the others and flying along a different path. They disappeared into the cloud cover after passing over the house.

The sighting lasted 10 minutes.

8:17 p.m. Christmas Eve. Lafayette, Louisiana:

12 similar objects were reported.

"Tonight, on Christmas Eve, my sister, my mother, my mother's boyfriend, and I all witnessed the same UFO sighting," the witness said in their report.

The witness's mother, an executive assistant at a helicopter company, and her mother's boyfriend, a lawyer, were outside when they shouted for the witness and their sister to come look at something.

"My sister and I ran outside, and my mom pointed up at the sky excitedly," they said. "We looked up and saw these orange/red orb looking objects in the sky. There were about twelve of them and they were gliding across the sky. It was completely silent, and they looked as if they were pulsating; they would get brighter and dimmer."

The orbs followed one another across the sky; some following closely to each other while others were in a triangle formation.

"The whole event lasted about two minutes and when they got about halfway across the sky, one by one they faded and disappeared," the witness said. "I've always believed in UFOs but seeing one in person made my jaw drop. I sat outside for thirty minutes after with the hopes of seeing it again, but they never reappeared."

8:50 p.m. Christmas Eve. Irvine, California:

A witness reported eight fireballs.

The red fireballs would reportedly appear so close that the witness "could take a shot at them" and hover overhead before the bright light would dim and then shut off.

"We could still see the UFO while it [flew] away, going [straight] up," the witness said.

Afterward, two more fireballs would appear, and the process would repeat.

This lasted for approximately 10 minutes.

10:30 p.m. Christmas Eve. San Antonio, Texas:

Two "bright orange lights" were reportedly seen.

"Two bright orange lights were moving straight across the sky with no engine sound," the witness said in their report.

They were out walking their dog when they saw the first light, which was moving from the northwest to the east.

As they turned back to the northwest to return to their house, they saw another bright orange light moving in the same pattern.

"I asked my family to come out and look at the light," they said. "We all thought the light appeared to be flickering but it was bright. It moved in a straight line following the same path as the previous light but there was no sound."

The sighting lasted around five minutes.

10:44 p.m. Christmas Eve. Spring Hill, Tennessee:

A witness reported three "hovering, orange, round objects" above the trees behind their apartment

They watched the objects, which emitted an "orange/amber glow," as they slowly flew away before disappearing into the clouds.

The objects made no sound.

The sighting lasted approximately three minutes.

11 p.m. Christmas Eve. Vista, California:

A witness was driving home with their family from a holiday get-together, when they said their wife pointed out twelve flying "orange glowing balls."

The fireballs flew in a two-wide by six-long formation and "just faded out" after five minutes.

No reported time. Christmas Day. Nashville, Georgia:

A witness reportedly saw an indeterminate number of orange lights traveling in a southeasterly direction. The objects didn't blink, nor did they make any sound.

They watched the lights until they moved out of sight.

Afterward, another orange light appeared that "was going relatively fast."

The witness speculated that the light appeared as though it was "trying to catch up with the other lights."

This sighting lasted approximately five minutes.

12:30 a.m. Christmas Day. Vista, California:

A witness and their family were driving home after celebrating Christmas Eve at their parents' house, when they saw "several bright colored orange balls of light floating north."

The lights were reportedly about a quarter mile in the air, made no noise, and left no contrails.

"My wife and I and our three boys were driving home from Christmas Eve at my parents' house," the witness said in their report.

"When we crested a small hill in the road, heading south on East Vista Way, we all saw several orange-colored balls of light floating or drifting along heading north over East Vista Way and Mason Street. There were about 10 to 12 of these balls, just slowly floating north toward us."

The witness asked their wife to pull over to film the event, but "she would not stop due to our scared and frightened kids."

She did finally relent and pulled over at the corner of Warmlands Avenue and East Vista Way, at which point the witness "jumped out just to see [the lights] turning off or disappearing."

Another motorist had also pulled over and asked them if they had seen the lights.

"He was very excited, as I was," the witness said. "I told him I did not know what they were. He jumped in his car and left, and we did the same, since the lights were gone."

In total, this sighting lasted around three minutes.

2 a.m. Christmas Day. Pickens, South Carolina:

A witness reported a "fire orb" first seen through the closed blinds of the back door to their parents' home.

They were on the couch, preparing to sleep, when an "intense orange glow" caught their attention.

At first, they thought that the glow might have been caused by a previously unknown lamp post between a cow pasture and nearby woods, despite having been familiar with the area for over two decades.

But upon closer inspection, the strange light seemed to be moving up and down and side to side.

The orange light appeared to be "touching down in the pasture and sending off some sort of electricity all around it."

After observing the phenomenon for 15 minutes, the witness "noticed a smaller white-blue orb hovering higher in the sky but keeping to the right."

The witness grabbed their phone to record what was happening, but as they did so, they realized that the orbs seemed to be aware they were being watched and would "shape shift" when the witness focused on them.

After an hour, the witness was frozen in fear and began to feel that they needed to hide.

"The red orb began to come as close as 20 feet from the back door," they said. "The fear that I felt was more real than anything else I can remember. So much that I was too terrified to even get up and wake up my parents or my brothers."

From that point to 6 a.m., there is a gap in their memory.

The next thing they know, they wake up in a cold sweat on the couch having forgotten what they'd just experienced. When their family awoke, the witness inexplicably showed them a video they'd recorded of the lights and said they had eventually discovered that it meant no harm to them and went to sleep.

"It wasn't for several days that I came out of the fog I was in to realize that I actually have no such memory of thinking that," they said.

Their family was at a loss to explain the events.

"To this day I have no explanation," they said. "I feel like something is definitely happening all around us and because not enough eyewitnesses have come forward, the general public is waving off these phenomena."

The duration of their sighting was three or more hours, although the lasting effects appear to be much longer.

6:45 p.m. Christmas Day. Hillsboro, Oregon:

A witness said they were sitting in their car in a parking lot when they noticed seven red lights hovering to the southwest before moving in different directions.
The lights reportedly made no sound.

"After about 30 seconds, I realized by the way they were moving, these were not airplanes," the witness said.

The sighting lasted around a minute.

7:03 p.m. Christmas Day. Glendora, California:

A witness reportedly encountered a fireball with a yellow center and amber-red edges while they and their mother were walking their dogs on South Vermont Avenue.
The fireball flew out of the Foothills of the San Gabriel Valley to the north at a distance and altitude that they estimated to be 35 yards away and 60 feet high, respectively.
It moved to the south, in the direction of and parallel to their position, as they were headed north on the west side of the street.
The witness said there was no vehicle, air, or pedestrian traffic in the area at the time.

Their surroundings were completely quiet, and the night sky was clear with no fog or rain.

The fireball made no sound as it quickly approached the pair at what the witness estimated to be 60 to 75 mph before coming to a stop next to them.

At that point, they were able to carefully examine the mysterious object.

While doing so, their dogs become agitated.

They also experienced difficulties when trying to use their cell phone.

"I called my girlfriend but was unable to make a connection; however, I then called my friend ... and was able to make a connection that faded in and out but strong enough to talk to him clearly," the witness said. "As we observed this fireball hovering with absolutely no sound next to us, I kept looking down at my watch to ensure there was no missing time. I continued to describe the event to my friend on the phone."

The witness's mother was becoming nervous, so they advised her not to look at the object as they continued to walk the dogs.

As they continued their walk, the fireball began to move again, slowly, at an estimated 30 mph, while making a loop to the southwest.

After about a quarter mile it "vanishes into thin air," making "no sound at all."

Approximately two minutes later the fireball returned, or perhaps a second fireball appeared, the witness said. The fireball flew along the same trajectory, but at half the altitude, only about 30 feet in the air.

"The fireball slowed to a crawl as it passed by us, and, just as it passed us, poof...gone," the witness said. "Afterwards I was able to make a connection on my cell phone with my girlfriend and told her all about our sighting."

The sighting lasted around eight minutes.

YULETIDE GUIDE TO HIGH STRANGENESS

7:10 p.m. Christmas Day. Newberg, Oregon:

A witness and their family reportedly saw a formation of orange orbs.

"I witnessed—along with my husband, my sister-in-law, and my two sons—eight to ten bright orange orbs moving very slowly in a ... formation," the witness said in their report. "I say formation because they seemed to move in an orderly fashion."

The orbs were "methodically spaced apart" from the south to the north, and disappeared as they headed east.

"Almost as if they were being blocked by something or entering something," the witness said.

This was reportedly the third "strange" sighting that the witness had experienced in their three years of residence in the area.

"I have always shoved them off as my eyes playing tricks on me. I am not a believer in aliens or any such thing. However, this was an incredibly strange event that I cannot (nor can anyone else with me) explain, so I thought it noteworthy enough to post," they said.

The sighting lasted approximately five minutes.

7:30 p.m. Christmas Day. Satellite Beach, Florida:

A witness reported "three bright orange objects" in the eastern/ southeastern sky seen while out walking their dog.

"They were stationary for a few minutes, then one quickly shot up and was gone. After about 15 seconds, the second one did the same. The third object remained for about a minute and then was gone," they said. "I see helicopters and planes here all the time and these objects were quiet and when they moved were beyond the speed of anything I have ever seen."

The sighting lasted around five minutes.

7:30 p.m. Christmas Day. Coral Springs, Florida:

Roughly 150 miles down Florida's coast from Satellite Beach, a witness reportedly saw three orange balls flying in formation after leaving their aunt's house for Christmas dinner.

The lights reportedly flew in formation for approximately two minutes before one broke off and disappeared midair, followed by the other two within 10 seconds.

7:35 p.m. Christmas Day. East Wenatchee, Washington:

A witness reported a "stationary orange light" over a ridge above Malaga, Washington, "where the big power lines come up from Rock Island Dam."

The witness said they had stepped out onto their porch and saw what they "first thought was a star low in the sky above the ridge across the Columbia River."

"My first thought was Sirius because it was sort of blinking quickly like that star does, only it was staying the same orangish color," they said. "It was about three times the size of Venus and a bit more orange than Mars, and it was stationary in the sky."

They called their daughter out to see the light, and as they were looking at it, it slowly diminished until it disappeared.

The light was in almost the same area as two gold balls of light that they had reported in the previous February.

The sighting lasted about two minutes.

9:15 p.m. Christmas Day. Davie, Florida:

A nursing home CEO and a psychotherapist reportedly witnessed an "orange glow" that was "twinkling occasionally."

This glow seemingly emanated from five silent orange lights, spaced out evenly, seen moving southwest.

The lights appeared to cross into the west flight path for planes landing at Fort Lauderdale.

"One light was near a plane preparing to land but the proximity of height was unknown as well as the height of the plane. The landing plane appeared to circle further out towards the south while landing east," they said.

Although they could not accurately estimate the lights' altitude, they were below the cloud ceiling.

The sighting lasted approximately five minutes.

9:30 p.m. Christmas Day. Kent, Washington:

A witness reported several silent reddish orange fireball-like lights streaking across the sky, barely above the trees.

The witness had just returned home from picking up their sister and was parking their car in the driveway. As they got out of the car, they noticed the anomalous low-flying fireballs.

"I quickly told my sister who was getting out of the car as well, and she looked up and saw what I was seeing. We watched them fly across the sky from the south heading north," they said. "After the first group went, I looked back and saw that more were approaching as well. The objects did not appear to be making any sound at all as they flew across the sky."

The pair watched as the lights flew by in the distance, until they grew smaller and smaller, eventually appearing like stars.

"I am not for sure, but it almost seemed like they were going upward into the sky at that point and not across," the witness said.

The witness's sister reportedly took pictures of the lights with her cell phone, which she posted to her Facebook page.

As for the witness who reported the anomalous fireballs, they were so startled by the experience that they called their family and friends to relate it.

The sighting lasted approximately five minutes.

10 p.m. Christmas Day. Cincinnati, Ohio:

A witness reported "five dancing fireballs" in the sky.

They said they were sitting in their car, warming it up before leaving for work, and when they reached over the passenger seat for their purse, they noticed five orange lights through the nearby trees.

One of the orange lights was alone, while the other four were next to each other in sets of two.

"My first thought was plane headlights, but they were orange/red and travelling too close to each other," the witness said.

They got out of their car when they saw the lights begin to move around each other, "almost dancing," and saw one of them slowly float upwards as it faded.

The witness ran into the house to get their brother, who came outside just in time to see the last two lights move upwards and fade away.

The sighting lasted less than five minutes.

11 p.m. Christmas Day. St. Petersburg Beach, Florida:

A witness reported a "bright ball of fire" moving east over the Gulf of Mexico.

"It's real," they said. "I saw and recorded it."

The witness was reportedly staying at the Grand Plaza Hotel on Gulf Boulevard in a room facing the ocean. Looking out the window, they saw a "bright ball of fire" appear, which "began moving east at a concentrated level of speed."

Stunned, they grabbed their cell phone and began recording video of the phenomenon as it moved upward and to the east until it "just vanished."

"I won't be the same," the witness said. "I know what I saw."

The sighting lasted around three minutes.

11 p.m. Christmas Day. Orangeburg, South Carolina:

A witness reported three orange lights in a triangle formation, pulsating left to right in an "intelligent manner."

Once they pointed out the lights, they faded away, one by one.

"I felt them making me aware of their presence," they said of the lights.

The sighting lasted approximately five minutes.

***

If these are the sightings that were reported, then we can only imagine how many went unreported.

So too can we imagine what it might have been like for our ancestors to witness such a spectacle. They likely struggled to contextualize what they were experiencing, and they could hardly be blamed for creating the Wild Hunt to explain events such as seeing mysterious orange lights or troops of little men or being abducted by otherworldly beings. And if we are tempted to judge them as somehow less discerning than us for these stories, we must first remind ourselves that contriving narratives to help explain such experiences is still widely practiced today. We struggle no less than they did to explain these events.

Experiencers and investigators alike have invented elaborate speculations—which all too often quickly become beliefs—to make sense of the often-nonsensical nature of the unknown. UFOs and associated phenomena alone have spawned everything from tales of sinister conspiracies and hybrid experiments to benevolent galactic federations. Yet we have no more evidence to prove the veracity of these narratives than we do for the Wild Hunt. I am certain that people experience things they cannot explain, just as I am sure that these phenomena—whatever they represent—have been with us throughout history. The one thing that appears to change is how we explain them.

SANTA'S LITTLE HELPERS

Before we move on to Santa, and since we were just discussing faerie troops and mysterious little men, now would seem as good a time as any to explore the origin of his elves.

There can be no discussion of Santa Claus without the inevitable inclusion of the context in which we understand him today. There is of course the North Pole, introduced into Santa's legendarium by political cartoonist Thomas Nast, who in the mid-19th century produced annual Christmas drawings featuring the fat man in what at the time was considered quite the adventurous locale. It was cold, which already fit with the kind of weather commonly associated with Santa and Christmas, but it was also remote, which meant very few people would be able to actually verify whether he was really up there—and thus an element of mystery was injected into the story.

And of course, there is Mrs. Claus, who was first mentioned in the short story *A Christmas Legend* by Christian missionary James Rees. Mrs. Claus is largely seen as a background character in the stories of Santa, although one with an interesting job. She is often depicted as being responsible for the care of Santa's reindeer and overseeing his elves.

While some attribute the addition of little elvish helpers to author Louisa May Alcott, this is not a settled literary fact, since the work in question, *Christmas Elves*, written in 1855, was never published and the manuscript has since been lost or destroyed. What we do know is that in 1857, American political magazine Harper's Weekly featured a poem in its Christmas edition, titled *The Wonders of Santa Claus*, which said that Santa:

Christmas Elf / Santa's Helper, illustration by Emily Wayland

Keeps a great many elves at work
All working with all their might
To make a million of pretty things
Cakes, sugar-plums and things
To fill the stockings, hung up you know,
By the little girls and boys...

And in 1873, Santa's elves were featured on the front cover illustration for the Christmas issue of *Godey's Lady's Book*, which came with the caption, "Here we have an idea of the preparations that are made to supply the young folks with toys at Christmas time." None of these depictions existed in a vacuum, of course, and they mixed freely with Scandinavian mythology like the álfar, also known as huldufólk or "hidden folk".

But to really explain how we got to the Christmas elves that we have today, we need to talk about gnomes.

Gnomes, as we know them today, appear as wizened old men with big, bushy beards wearing tall, red hats—identical to folkloric little men known as nisser (singular nisse) in Danish and Norwegian or tomtar (singular tomte) in Swedish. But they didn't start out that way. The word gnome itself comes from the Renaissance Latin *gnomus* (possibly derived from the Latin gēnomos, or "earth-dweller"), and was coined by Paracelsus for his work *Liber de Nymphis, Sylvanis, Pygmaeis, Salamandrix, et Gigantibus, etc.*, published posthumously in 1566. Paracelsus—a Swiss physician, alchemist, and astrologer—classified gnomes as earth elementals, and likely drew upon stories from his Germanic homeland of little men who lived below ground, like dwarfs, when forming his idea of them.

Traditionally, gnomes live underground. Paracelsus described them as "two spans [the distance from the tip of the thumb to the tip of the little finger when one's hand is outstretched] high" and said that they can move through the earth as a man moves through air. So, too, do the nisser and tomtar, who are short, helpful household faeries who attach to specific homesteads or families and are often said to dwell underground in the foundations of old homes and in burial mounds. This tradition stems from the belief that they're the ancestral spirits of ancient family patriarchs, which explains their wizened, gray appearance. In general, these faeries are known for bringing more weal than woe, at least if they respect those with whom they dwell.

Nisser, illustration by Emily Wayland

Nisser are extremely strong for their size and use their strength to both help with chores and act as guardians of the homes they place under their protection. It's important to respect a nisse's wishes and live a good, productive life, as well as generally being polite to the house gnome, or he will become offended and seek retribution that can take the form of anything from minor pranks to ruining the offending party's fortunes completely. Being polite to a nisse includes such considerations as yelling a warning if one should spill anything in the house, and not urinating anywhere other than the toilet—one never knows where a nisse might be standing.

Nisser love animals in general, but horses specifically; it's said that one can tell which horse in a stable is a nisse's favorite, since it will always appear the most nourished and well-groomed. Similar to brownies, a gift of food can go a long way towards improving a nisse's temperament, and they particularly enjoy a good bowl of porridge topped with butter. Nisser are especially active around Yule, when they deliver presents at the doors of their adopted homesteads.

Although always described as humanoid in appearance, it wasn't until the 18th century that gnomes were popularly portrayed with the bushy beards and red hats that have made them synonymous with nisser and tomtar, and by the 19th century they were indistinguishable. Furthermore, by the 1700s, it was a popular custom in Switzerland to decorate one's home with gnomes, further strengthening their connection with the nisser and tomtar by establishing them as household spirits. This practice continues today worldwide with garden gnomes and other small gnomish statuary often found in and around people's homes.

It was the nisser (and by extension, the gnomes who had adopted their appearance) who, already associated with Yule, most influenced early writers and artists when Santa's elves were first being introduced in the 19th century—which brings us full circle to why the elves are so often depicted as short, hardworking old men with white beards and colorful, conical hats.

JOLLY OLD ST. NICHOLAS

So far, we've discussed a variety of monstrous interlopers who are intent on ruining Christmas for anyone caught unawares, but not all such visitors during the holidays are unfriendly. In fact, one of them we welcome annually with open arms despite his close resemblance to the home invaders and abductors associated with the Wild Hunt. I'm referring, of course, to Santa Claus.

Santa Claus gets his name from Saint Nicholas, or more accurately, from the Dutch Sinterklaas (literally Dutch for Saint Nicholas).

Saint Nicholas was simply Nicholas when he was born in third century Greece. The future saint was raised as a devout Christian by his wealthy parents, and when they died in his youth, Nicholas decided to emulate Jesus and use his inheritance to help the needy. He dedicated his life to the Church and was eventually made Bishop of Myra while still a young man. Bishop Nicholas was known for his generosity, love of children, and concern for sailors and ships.

The popular Christian bishop was persecuted by the Roman Emperor Diocletian, who imprisoned and exiled Nicholas. Bishop Nicholas is said to have attended the Council of Nicaea in 325 AD and died eighteen years later in 343 AD. Saint Nicholas was interred in his cathedral, where it is claimed a special liquid relic with great healing properties—called manna—formed in his grave. The supposed formation of this mysterious manna did much to encourage his veneration.

The centuries following Saint Nicholas's death saw the wide circulation of many stories surrounding his miraculous deeds. One such story that relates specifically to gift-giving during the holiday season

St. Nicholas, illustration by Emily Wayland

is that, on three separate occasions, Saint Nicholas tossed bags of gold through the windows of a poor man to provide a dowry for the man's daughters, lest they be forced to become prostitutes.

According to Michael the Archimandrite's *Life of Saint Nicholas*—thought to be the earliest and first complete record of the saint's life, written in the 9th century—there was a "recently famous and well-born" man who was once a neighbor of Nicholas. Unfortunately, "owing to the plotting and envy of Satan," the man had gone from wealth to extreme poverty. However, the man had three "shapely and very attractive" daughters whom he planned to force into prostitution to fund his lifestyle, since nobody was willing to marry them lawfully; not even someone among the lower classes. So, frustrated, he gave up on looking to God for help through persistence and prayer, and went with prostituting his daughters.

But apparently, the Lord did not want to see this man "become hostage to sin," so Nicholas was sent to "rescue him, along with his whole household, from poverty and destruction, and to restore readily his previous prosperity." Nicholas was reminded of several salient Bible passages upon hearing of the family's plight. "God loves a person who is a cheerful giver" (Proverbs 22.8), "The one who pities a beggar is himself nurtured" (Proverbs 22.9), "Provide good things before God and humankind" (Proverbs 3.4), and "Save those who are led away to death (Proverbs 24.11). Thus, Nicholas was inspired to generously donate his own money to save the family from a life of sinful dissolution.

Nicholas decided that his help must come surreptitiously, because he did not want to shame the man, nor did he want to "trumpet his own charity." So, he hurled a bag containing a large amount of gold into their house through the window at night, after which he rushed home. The next day, the man found the bag that Nicholas had left and "he was seized with joy and with ungovernable tears and gave thanks to God with amazement and astonishment, wondering in himself from where so great a blessing had come to him." The amount of gifted gold was sufficient to act as a dowry, and so the man "without delay contrived a marriage for his first daughter, having acquired for her an honorable life with joy and pleasure granted by the mediation of Saint Nicholas."

When Nicholas saw that the first gift had resulted in a wedding for the man's first daughter, he went back on a subsequent night and threw another bag of gold, equal to the previous one, through the same window, after which he again hastened to his own home. Again, the man found this gift the next morning and was stunned at his good fortune, "giving prayers of thanksgiving to God with groans (as is reasonable), unable to wholly open his mouth to him because he was struck dumb at the doubling of his kindness." When he found his voice, the man cried out to God to show him the "angel among men" responsible for the gold, since it would allow him to give another of his daughters a lawful marriage, "freeing her from the impiety which we formerly practiced, because of our unexpected desperation."

After that, the father resolved to stay awake and vigilant the following nights, "confidently expecting that the person who had secretly furnished such money for her sisters would provide the dowry for his third daughter." And, sure enough, as the man sat up one night, fighting drowsiness, Nicholas came and again threw a similar gift of gold through the same window, withdrawing quietly afterward.

But this time the man was ready for him and became suddenly aware as the gold was tossed inside his window. He gave chase and overtook Nicholas at a run. When he caught the saint, "he threw himself face first at his feet with cries and gave thanks to him over and over with many words and called him, his and his three daughters' savior."

"If our common Master, Christ, hadn't stirred your goodness, we would have long ago destroyed our own lives by a shameful and destructive livelihood," he said to Nicholas. "But as it is, the Lord has saved us through you, most blessed one, and rescued us from the filth of immorality. And so we ought, like a debt, to give thanks to you all of our days, because you stretched out a hand of help to us and caused the poor to rise from the ground and raised the destitute up from a dunghill through your generous and truly wonderful gift."

But when Saint Nicholas heard these words, "he raised him up from the ground and, binding him by an oath not to make any of these blessings, of which he had thought him worthy, known to anyone for as long as he should live, he let him go in peace."

This story sets a very early precedent for what would evolve into the secretive nocturnal activities of Santa Claus on Christmas Eve.

By the Middle Ages, giving gifts during the feast of Saint Nicholas had become a popular activity, and children would leave a stocking or shoe out the night before, on December 5th, in the hopes that by morning it might be filled with treats.

But with the Reformation in 16th century Europe, came significant pushback to the veneration of saints, and this tradition of gift giving was moved to the day earmarked for the celebration of Christ: Christmas Day.

This same period brought Father Christmas to England, a festive spirit clad in green or red fur-lined robes who embodied the good cheer of the season.

But before them all came Odin.

Odin, with his long white beard and cloak who rides his eight-legged horse Sleipnir to lead the Wild Hunt during Yule. And Yule, of course, was moved to coincide with the same date that people now celebrate Christmas.

In her 1968 book *Discovering Christmas Customs and Folklore: A Guide to Seasonal Rites Throughout the World*, folklorist Margaret Baker wrote, "The appearance of Santa Claus or Father Christmas, whose day is 25th December, owes much to Odin, the old blue-hooded, cloaked, white-bearded Giftbringer of the north, who rode the midwinter sky on his eight-footed steed Sleipnir, visiting his people with gifts. Minor solstitial deities went with him. Gradually the lesser gods were lost, but Odin transformed into Father Christmas, then Santa Claus, prospered and with St. Nicholas and the Christchild became a leading player on the Christmas stage."

Baker went on to write, "It was in the United States that modern Santa Claus evolved, blending Old Father Christmas from England, the St. Nicholas of Hessian troops and Dutch immigrants—and more than a hint of the rotund, smiling elf of northern Europe."

An early example of this amalgamation—one that is still a perennial Christmas favorite, in fact—is the beloved 1822 poem by Clement Clarke Moore entitled *A Visit from St. Nicholas*, more popularly known today as *The Night Before Christmas*.

'Twas the night before Christmas, when all through the house
Not a creature was stirring, not even a mouse;
The stockings were hung by the chimney with care,
In hopes that St. Nicholas soon would be there;

The children were nestled all snug in their beds,
While visions of sugar-plums danced in their heads;
And mamma in her 'kerchief, and I in my cap,
Had just settled our brains for a long winter's nap,

When out on the lawn there arose such a clatter,
I sprang from the bed to see what was the matter.
Away to the window I flew like a flash,
Tore open the shutters and threw up the sash.

The moon on the breast of the new-fallen snow
Gave the lustre of mid-day to objects below,
When, what to my wondering eyes should appear,
But a miniature sleigh, and eight tiny reindeer,
With a little old driver, so lively and quick,
I knew in a moment it must be St. Nick.

More rapid than eagles his coursers they came,
And he whistled, and shouted, and called them by name;
"Now, Dasher! now, Dancer! now, Prancer and Vixen!
On, Comet! on, Cupid! on, Donner and Blitzen!
To the top of the porch! to the top of the wall!
Now dash away! dash away! dash away all!"

As dry leaves that before the wild hurricane fly,
When they meet with an obstacle, mount to the sky;
So up to the house-top the coursers they flew,
With the sleigh full of Toys, and St. Nicholas too.
And then, in a twinkling, I heard on the roof
The prancing and pawing of each little hoof.

As I drew in my head, and was turning around,
Down the chimney St. Nicholas came with a bound.
He was dressed all in fur, from his head to his foot,
And his clothes were all tarnished with ashes and soot;
A bundle of Toys he had flung on his back,
And he looked like a peddler just opening his pack.

His eyes—how they twinkled! his dimples how merry!
His cheeks were like roses, his nose like a cherry!
His droll little mouth was drawn up like a bow
And the beard of his chin was as white as the snow;
The stump of a pipe he held tight in his teeth,
And the smoke it encircled his head like a wreath;

Santa Claus, illustration by Emily Wayland

He had a broad face and a little round belly,
That shook when he laughed, like a bowlful of jelly.
He was chubby and plump, a right jolly old elf,
And I laughed when I saw him, in spite of myself;

A wink of his eye and a twist of his head,
Soon gave me to know I had nothing to dread;
He spoke not a word, but went straight to his work,
And filled all the stockings; then turned with a jerk,
And laying his finger aside of his nose,
And giving a nod, up the chimney he rose;
He sprang to his sleigh, to his team gave a whistle,
And away they all flew like the down of a thistle,
But I heard him exclaim, ere he drove out of sight,
"Happy Christmas to all, and to all a good-night."

This poem would inform our opinions on Santa Claus for over a century, but it was illustrator Haddon Sundblom who really cemented the image of a plump, jolly man with rosy cheeks, clad in red, and sporting a bushy white beard.

Sundblom was commissioned by Coca-Cola to create a wholesome image of Santa for an advertising campaign, and his employers wanted something unlike the illustrations of an often-gaunt man or small, elflike creature that had been in circulation prior. He was heavily influenced in his work by A Visit from St. Nicholas and the campaign was a huge success, which is how we came to have the iconic image of Santa Claus that we do today.

This is important, because in addition to influencing the public image of Santa Claus, it's shaped the perception of those who have claimed to see him in real life.

HERE COMES SANTA CLAUS

In 2021, I received the following report from Haley Pearce, then 24, who said that when she was eight years old, she had stepped outside of the Christmas Eve service at her local church in Lancaster, Ohio, only to see what appeared to be a sleigh pulled by reindeer flying overhead.

When I was a kid, I absolutely believed in Santa Claus. As much as a kid possibly could. So much so, in fact, that I wanted to BE Santa when I grew up. I believed in Santa a lot later than I probably should have—I was in 6th grade before I finally lost the spirit, and I think a lot of that has to do with my experience.

I was probably 8 years old, and we were leaving the 11p.m. Christmas Eve service at our church in Lancaster, Ohio. I had been obsessively tracking Santa on the NORAD website all day and was looking forward to getting home so I could crawl into bed and stay up as late as possible; listening for sleigh bells or hooves on our roof, like I did every year.

I was the first person out of the church when the service was over, because what little kid wants to stay in church on Christmas Eve? It was a clear, cold night, and the stars were gorgeous. So, I was admiring the stars when I saw a kind of shimmering out of the corner of my eye. I looked and saw what I can only describe as Santa's sleigh. It looked just like it does in every movie. It was pulled by reindeer, and it left a trail of glowing glitter behind it that faded quickly. I don't remember if I heard sleigh bells or not.

It happened so fast, but I was absolutely SURE of what

I saw. I kind of stood there in shock until my parents came out. I told them what I had seen, and they basically said "Well, we'd better get home and get to bed so he doesn't skip our house."

Over the years, I kind of began to doubt my sighting; chalked it up to a shooting star and wishful thinking. But as I've gotten older and become more open-minded about the nature of the universe and the paranormal, I've accepted my experience for what it was. It was Santa's sleigh.

I was able to follow up with Haley, who agreed to answer questions about her sighting.

Haley told me that she was alone outside during the sighting, and that the event lasted "probably five seconds."

"I swear I saw a person inside the sleigh, but I couldn't make out any details on them or on the sleigh," she said. "It all happened so fast."

Haley added she doesn't remember anything else unusual happening around that time but has experienced several other UFO encounters and minor paranormal events.

"Nothing else unusual happened around then that I can remember, but it was so long ago, and I was so young," she explained. "I have had three UFO encounters, including one where everyone in my family and I saw a black triangle. A few unexplainable things have happened to me at home, too, but mostly little things that aren't too exciting unless you were there."

She went on to explain that, although she was, admittedly, "a very imaginative little kid," she didn't have any conditions that would lead to hallucinations and was "quite sure" about what she saw.

"I know I didn't imagine it," she said. "The only other possible explanation I can think of is that it was a meteor, but I really don't think it was."

Although rare, at least one researcher has claimed to have collected other stories of Santa Claus sightings.

Stephen Wagner posted a list of over a dozen such sightings, updated most recently in 2019, to the website *LiveAbout*.

The witnesses in these encounters are, unsurprisingly, almost exclusively children, with the lone outlier being a sighting of what was, in all likelihood, a perfectly normal human being.

The sighting reports are either partially or entirely anonymous and generally describe up-close encounters with Santa Claus inside of the witness's home.

Although some of the sightings listed by Wagner likely have prosaic explanations, there are several that are noteworthy in our examination of Santa Claus sightings as a potentially paranormal phenomenon.

Often these entries include only a first name, sometimes accompanied by a last initial, which I have included in the assumption that they are accurate and represent real people. Dates and locations have also been included when available. As with anything else that has not been verified, please take these accounts with a grain of salt. They are strictly for comparative purposes in our phenomenological examination of Santa Claus.

Location Unknown, 1969:

"Joanne" wrote that she was just three years old when she came downstairs one Christmas morning, excited to see what Santa had brought her, only to find her parents hanging around with "an old guy with a white beard and hair with a red suit."

She ran back to her room as fast as she could, and didn't mention the incident until years later, when she told her mother what she had seen. Joanne's mother insisted that either she had been dreaming or somehow misidentified her own father, but Joanne didn't think that was possible, since her father had been sitting in a chair behind the stranger and her mother was standing next to him.

"I'm African American," she added, "and during that time the tenants in our building were all African American, so Santa stood out!"

Location Unknown, 1973:

"Del" wrote about how, one Christmas Eve, while they were in their teens, they were in a car with their parents, having just returned home for the night. During the ride, they had been talking about Santa

Claus, and "how great it would be if he really did exist."

Then, as they pulled into their driveway, they saw him, Santa, tiptoeing in the snow between two houses across the street. According to Del, the family "all laughed when we saw this and remembered the incident for many Christmases thereafter."

And lest one think that this may have been some holiday mischief maker out to make trouble, Del made sure to add that no robberies had been reported following their sighting.

Scotland, 1978:

"Jimmy" wrote about an experience he and an old friend had shared. At around 7:30 p.m. on a clear Christmas Eve night, the two "suddenly heard a bell or bells in the distance getting closer real fast."

As they looked up, they saw Santa in his sleigh being pulled by reindeer as they flew "very fast and low" over Jimmy's house.

"It was brief, but we both ran to tell our families," Jimmy said. "Of course, everyone laughed, but I tell you it was real!"

Jimmy said that he and his friend had lost touch years ago, but that the friend had (recently to when the story was first shared) managed to track him down and brought him a Christmas card. He asked his friend if he remembered the sighting and the friend said that "of course he did ... but he didn't like telling people about it now."

"You can imagine why!" Jimmy added.

Memphis, Tennessee, 1980s and 2009:

"Mrs. Wages" wrote first of a strange sighting had sometime in the 1980s when she was eight or nine years old. She and her parents were arriving home to their house in the suburbs from a Christmas party on Christmas Eve when they saw Santa Claus hovering over their house in his sleigh.

"All we could hear were sleigh bells," Mrs. Wages said.

The sleigh was reportedly illuminated, which allowed them to see Santa, resplendent in his red and white outfit.

Although she said she remembers seeing reindeer, Mrs. Wages does not know how many there were.

After a moment of the stunned family taking in this bizarre event, Santa merely waved at them before flying away.

"I'll never forget it, and I'll never forget my dad's face of total shock," Mrs. Wages said. "He was an air traffic controller and when he went back to work after the holidays, he asked about it and nothing came up."

Decades later, on Black Friday in 2009, Mrs. Wages said that she was at the local Target store when she began a conversation with another woman in line.

"We were talking about Christmas shopping, and all of a sudden out of nowhere she mentioned that her brother had seen Santa Claus in his sleigh two years before," she said. "I stood with my mouth wide open because I couldn't believe it. Every Christmas Eve I still think about him and look outside to try to get a glimpse."

Bristol, England, 2000:

"Alex H." wrote that, at about midnight on Christmas Eve, they heard "these big footsteps" coming from the living room, accompanied by "bells tingling" from somewhere above.

Alex's parents and sister were also present in the house at the time, although only Alex was awake, having been unable to sleep due to excitement.

Although they were "quite scared," Alex decided to investigate the footsteps.

"I walked down the stairs very slowly and I could see this big man putting presents around my living room," Alex said. "I wanted to say something, but I was too scared to do it because I thought he would be angry."

Instead of interrupting, Alex ran back upstairs and went back to bed.

"I was so convinced I saw the real Santa and told everyone in the morning, but no one believed me," they said.

Alex said that they were 14 at the time of writing about their experience, but without knowing when that was, it's difficult to extrapolate their current age.

Although, presumably, they were a relatively young child at the time of their sighting.

New York City, 2002, 2004, and 2007:

"Claxton Kalmbach" wrote that he had his first sighting of a strange Yuletide visitor in 2002.

Claxton had gone upstairs that Christmas Eve following a celebration of family and friends that his parents had invited to their home. While everyone else was in the living room watching a movie, Claxton found himself pacing by himself back and forth in the hallway, having no interest in the movie downstairs and having found nothing worthwhile to watch on the television in his room.

After "about seven minutes" of pacing, Claxton said, "I saw a tall, fat figure scurry away about 20 feet away from me. It was crouched down, too. It was even wearing some sort of Santa Claus suit."

Claxton didn't believe in Santa and was understandably concerned at the thought of a strange man in the house.

He ran downstairs to tell his parents, but they simply grinned at him and said, jokingly, "Maybe it was Santa Claus."

That explanation did little to comfort Claxton, so he opted to join everyone in the living room for the remainder of the evening.

His next encounter came on Christmas Eve of 2004, and this experience, Claxton said, left an even more indelible impression.

He was lying on the couch in the living while his parents were conversing in the kitchen, when suddenly, he saw "a huge man, about seven or eight feet tall, crawl underneath the tree and just vanish."

Before the bulky stranger disappeared, he looked at Claxton and said, "Shh."

Deciding that this event was too strange for him to remain comfortable alone, he went to join his parents in the kitchen.

These sightings became a regular occurrence, according to Claxton.

"I recall one in 2007, it was daylight this time and I just happened to see another tall figure with a Santa hat trudge by me for two seconds, then it was gone," he said. "This really happened!"

Location Unknown, 2003:

"Jade" wrote that, although she was 13 years old at the time of writing, she was only seven when she experienced her anomalous yuletide event.

While lying in bed awake at around midnight on Christmas Eve, she saw "a red light beaming down" into her window from the darkness outside.

"It was so bright, and somehow, I knew it was him," she said.

Jade looked up into the sky in the hopes of seeing Santa Claus, but all she saw was the bright light coming from a small object.

"I didn't hear a helicopter or anything, but I did hear the unique sound of bells and, of course, the sound of hooves tapping on the roof," she said. "These sounds lasted for a few seconds after the light had disappeared, then they were gone."

Location Unknown, 2006:

This story comes from a witness who chose to remain anonymous. They wrote about how, several Christmases ago, they were crying as they returned home from their aunt's holiday party, because one of their cousins had told them that Santa wasn't real.

When they turned onto their street, they saw a big red sleigh pulled by reindeer sitting on their roof, and as they watched, Santa then popped out of their chimney.

The next morning, this witness reportedly asked everyone else who was present (presumably their immediate family) if they remembered the sighting, but none of them did.

However, a couple of days ago, the witness said, "my dad went up to fix a leak … and there were long, straight lines going across the roof."

"I took a picture and showed it to my baby cousins and told them, 'Always believe,'" they added.

That picture was not included in Wagner's post on *LiveAbout*.

San Antonio:

"Drew" wrote that he was "about seven" when he saw something anomalous while looking outside of his second-story window, waiting to see Santa Claus.

"I saw something approaching in the distance: it was a huge sleigh, and it was flying right over my house! I don't remember seeing any reindeer, but I did see a man dressed in red with a beard," he said. "I was so startled, but I kept looking, even sticking my head and half my body outside of the window!"

Like so many others, Drew told his family, but felt as though they didn't really believe him.

"I swear on my life to this day I saw something. I don't know if it was really Santa Claus, but I did see what I described!" he said of the experience.

Australia:

"Nick" wrote about two strange experiences that he's willing to believe might be evidence of Santa Claus.

The first, he said, took place at his family's suburban home when he was about ten years old.

"I swear that on one Christmas Eve, I was sleeping in my room when I heard my backyard door open, then close, and then a minute later it opened and closed again another three times each, about a minute apart," he said. "I thought it must have been my parents bringing in our presents from our garage, although, I don't recall seeing them go past my bedroom to their room. I was hiding under the covers at the time."

Then, on another Christmas Eve, Nick decided to sneak down to the living room and catch Santa in the act of delivering presents but lost his nerve.

As he was walking back to his bedroom, he passed by the front door and the light came on from outside.

"I thought I could see the shadow of someone outside," Nick said. "Of course, now that I think about it, it could have just been a passerby or a cat or something. Or maybe—just maybe—it could have been Santa."

Location Unknown:

"Ana" wrote about how, when she was five years old, she heard a shuffling in the living room from her bedroom.

Curious, she peered cautiously around the doorway, only to see a man in a Santa suit standing in front of the family Christmas tree.

"He must have felt my presence because he turned around and looked at me," she said. "He didn't look jolly or kind and happy like you would expect Santa Claus to look. He looked kind of eerie like he was staring into my soul."

Naturally unnerved, Ana fled to her parents' room and hid under the covers.

"I don't know why I was so scared at the time, but I wrote it off as a dream for a while before I forgot about it completely," she said. "Years later, I remembered it. I thought it could have been a burglar, but when I asked my parents, nothing was ever missing from that apartment. The only time we were ever robbed was when we moved later on. The only explanation I have now is that it was some kind of apparition."

Location Unknown:

"Richard" wrote about a Santa Claus encounter he had when he was around eight years old.

It was close to midnight, and he had been lying awake in bed for about 30 minutes, unable to sleep due to his excitement over the presents he would receive in the morning.

As he lay there, he began to hear faint footsteps approaching, until, as he said, "Slowly, a man in boots, carrying a sack looked into my room, my parents' room and then my brother's room."

Richard could see the man well, because of the illumination of a nightlight across the hall in the bathroom.
He cautiously hid his face under a blanket with only a small portion of his eyes uncovered, so he could see, as the man walked quietly away and was gone.

Certain that he had been awake during the encounter, Richard told his parents and brother the next morning what had happened, but they didn't believe him.

"To this day (I'm 28 now), I ask my parents if they had anything to do with this, and they still deny it and say I was dreaming," he said. "I strongly believe I saw a spirit or some kind of entity of Santa."

***

But not all benevolent Yuletide visitors appear as the commercialized form of Santa Claus to which we've become accustomed. Some of them vary considerably from that jovial, rotund spirit, although their gifts are no less welcome for it. The figure in the following account is more reminiscent of Saint Nicholas than anything commissioned by Coca-Cola.

Tree was 57 when I spoke to her in 2022, but her first experience with holiday magic came when she was much younger.

It was the first week of January 1991. Tree was 26 and she was at a grocery store in Easton, Pennsylvania, with her then husband.

They found themselves counting their change at 1 a.m., dead sober and desperate to afford everything they needed.

"I eloped in 1990," Tree said in her initial email. "My very young husband and I moved away from my home and my family to live in eastern Pennsylvania, a place where he spent time as a child. We had no idea what we were doing. We moved without a place to live, without jobs and without a plan."

In the winter of that year, we had scraped together enough money to get an apartment but paying the rent left us without money for anything else. And my husband smoked. He didn't want to smoke, but nicotine addiction is the worst, and I couldn't stand to watch him when he couldn't get a cigarette. (Did I mention I was really young?)

In the middle of one night, we find ourselves in the back of the neighborhood's grocery store. The store was open 24 hours, and it was about 1 o'clock in the morning. We are standing next to the milk cooler, literally counting out pennies to see if we could swing a small carton of milk, a cheap loaf of bread, and some tobacco. We can't. I know we don't have enough money, and I am insisting we skip the bread and get milk and tobacco. My husband is insisting we need the food, and he can deal without smoking.

The guy came out of nowhere. We were standing in the back aisle of the store, which was wide and in the middle of a cold winter's night, empty. But suddenly there is a tall, thin, bald man in a long coat standing right next to us. There was no way he should have gotten so close without us noticing, but we were distracted by our situation.

Without so much as a "hello," this guy grasps my husband's hand and begins pouring change into it. My husband quickly lifted his other hand to try to catch all the money flowing out of this guy's leather pouch. (Who the hell carries change in a leather pouch tied with a cord?) All I could do was stare. As the change fills my husband's cupped hands, the guy laughs, saying "Buy some candy bars, too." And he winks at us.

I glance at my husband and down at the money and then up to say, "Thank you," but there is no one there. No one anywhere. There was nowhere he could have gone that quickly that we would not have been able to see him. The guy just vanished.

People I have told this story tell me none of this proves it was Santa Claus. But I know. All these years later, I still know. And we got everything we needed, and a couple chocolate bars, too.

I spoke to Tree over the phone after that.

"I know that it was shortly after Christmas. It wasn't on Christmas. Even 24-hour grocery stores in Pennsylvania aren't open on Christmas—or at least they weren't back then," she told me. "We were in the grocery store in the middle of the night, which was not uncommon for us because we were young."

The grocery store was empty, with only a cashier up front and maybe a couple of stock people around that the couple didn't see.

"That was one of the reasons the encounter was so strange, because the grocery store was so empty," she explained.

Despite his relatively brief manifestation, the mystery man left an indelible impression on Tree, and she still remembers the details of his appearance.

"I'm only five foot five. I remember that he was taller than us. I remember that I looked up at him when I first realized he was there. [He was] maybe a few inches over six feet. I know that he was bald. And he was wearing a long coat, like it buttoned up in the front, but it was a long coat that went all the way down to his calves. The coat was dark. He was Caucasian and he had the bluest eyes I've ever seen," she said. "I don't remember any facial hair. I'm not particularly great with faces, but I don't remember any [facial hair]."

As for his age, she said, "It felt like he was older. Well, older than us. We were in our early, early twenties. He was older than us."

The strangeness of his sudden disappearance stuck with Tree, since there simply wasn't anywhere that he could have gone in the time it took them to glance back up.

"The back aisle of the grocery store was one of those wide back aisles. It had the dairy cooler and the cakes and stuff, and we were actually in the back corner because that's where the milk was. So, we could see straight down to the front of the store to our right because that was the aisle all the way down to the front, and we could see all the way down the aisle along the back of the store. There were no people," she said. "I don't know where he could have come from. There were no doors that I remember, and we would have heard that. And even had he come around the corner from another aisle, it seems like I would have noticed that. It felt like he came out of nowhere."

"The showing up was less startling than when he let go of my ex-husband's hand and we were looking down at the money and looked up at each other and looked at him to thank him and he was just gone. At that moment, I thought, 'This is really weird. Where did he go?' There's nowhere he could have gone," she continued. "He would have had to walk at least 12 or 15 feet to an aisle that we couldn't see down."

Tree told me that she normally doesn't talk about this sort of thing but was intrigued by the oddity of my request for holiday stories.

"It was your request for a holiday thing. I was like, 'Yeah, okay, I guess I could tell this story,'" she said. "The older I get, the less easy it is to tell. People don't want to hear that somebody in their fifties believes in Santa."

That kindly older man playing the part of St. Nick in the grocery store wasn't the only Christmas miracle experienced by Tree.

"I will say this, every year since then, when I have not had any money or been in financial trouble, somebody has always shown up to give my kids gifts or give me a gift—somebody I don't know or somebody unexpected—ever since then," she said. "There were a couple of years that were very tough when my kids were very young. We lived in a trailer in the woods, not in a trailer park, way off the beaten path. We'd get up and there would be a laundry basket full of Christmas presents on the back step for the kids. Nobody even knows where we are. Where did that come from?"

However, she said, "I'm pretty sure it was people, not Santa Claus."

A different year, also around Christmastime, Tree was treated to another act of generosity.

"There was one year, I was in a bookstore looking at books and I didn't have any money to buy books," she said. "This woman literally walked up to me and said, 'I'll buy those for you,' and she took them out of my arms and walked them up to the register, bought them, and brought them to me with a receipt. She said, 'Enjoy,' and walked out of the store."

"Never saw her before, never saw her again. That was just a thing that happened," Tree added.

Regardless of whether one believes that any supernatural forces were at work here, the effect that these events have had on Tree is as undeniable as it is heartwarming.

"I think most people are really good, honestly. And now that I'm in a better place financially, I've started trying to do that for others. People who don't know me. It makes people smile. That's always fun," she told me. "That's what Santa Claus taught me at the end of the day, because of that first encounter and the following encounters, now it's a thing that I like to do."

Oddly enough, Santa Claus isn't the only legendary being associated with a holiday to have been reported to us directly at The Singular Fortean Society.

Our first report of an Easter Bunny sighting came in the form of an email received on January 10th, 2022.

It was titled, *Strange Encounter on Easter*.

Hello! I saw your posting looking for strange holiday encounters and stories. I've never gone on record with this story, but I can still picture it in my head as clear as the day it happened. I don't tell many people this story as it's often met with ridicule or disbelief, but I can swear on a stack of bibles that I remember it happening.

It happened when I was a child. I'm 28 now so I must have maybe been seven years old or younger at the time. I was very young. I would say maybe 1999 or 2000 but I'm not fully sure. I remember it was Easter morning. I was on the floor of my parents' living room watching some Easter special, playing with whatever new toy I got in my Easter basket, and feasting upon chocolate goodies.

I can clearly remember not hearing any sort of sound or something that would draw my attention, yet I looked out the sliding glass door of the living room that went to the fenced-in backyard. We lived in a residential neighborhood on a busy street with numerous neighbors around. So, we weren't out in the sticks by any means.

As I looked out the sliding glass door, I saw a flash of color. I distinctly remember white and blue and purple. I got up and looked out the window and saw something I'll never forget. Jumping over the fence into our backyard was a six-to-seven-foot-tall rabbit-man. It had the face of a rabbit with those cold darting eyes and twitching nose. Ears up and tall. White to cool blue/purple coloring in the fur. It didn't have an Easter basket or anything funny like that. It stood on two legs which were flat like a rabbit's hind legs with large powerful haunches. I don't remember what exactly the arms looked like, but I remember it held them close to its body. It jumped over the fence from the neighbor's house and landed in our yard. I stood there in awe as this thing hopped across the backyard. It stood for a second and looked at

Easter Bunny, illustration by Emily Wayland

me and proceeded to jump over the adjacent fence into the next neighbor's yard. That was the last I saw of it.

I immediately told my parents of what I saw, and they laughed and said I've watched too many Easter specials. They confirmed with me there was nobody running around the neighborhood in an Easter bunny costume. This was broad daylight, so it was odd that nobody else took notice of this thing. Maybe I was the only one who could see it?

I'm an avid cryptozoological investigator and have gone on numerous Sasquatch expeditions and have had what I believe to be a few encounters through the years. I've spent numerous field hours looking for UFOs and going on ghost hunts and things like that. Yet this always stuck in the back of my mind the most out of anything.

Thank you for reading this! Let me know if you have any questions or feedback! Like I said I am 100% honest and sincere in writing this.

I scheduled a phone interview with the witness to discuss their experience, but unfortunately, they said that they needed to cancel the interview and any subsequent attempts to reschedule were met with no response.

This emailed report would prove to be fruitful, however, as it led directly to the next report.

I had published it under the 'Reports from the Void' column we sometimes run in the news portion of our website.

As is explained in bold in the body of every article published to that column:

"Reports from the Void is a repository to share those stories for which we do not have enough information to make a full report. This is usually because of little or no communication from the witness following their initial submission. The Singular Fortean Society will always provide as much information as possible regarding any correspondence during our attempts to speak with those involved. This series is meant only to present you with the full breadth of the information sent to us and makes no judgments towards the veracity of any stories shared within it."

The Singular Fortean Society was contacted only days after publishing that 'Reports from the Void' article by Sharon, an Illinois woman who said that when she was eight or nine years old, she awoke early on Easter morning to see a six-foot-tall, white, bipedal rabbit wearing a black vest embroidered with multicolored glass beads hopping through her backyard.

When Sharon decided to reach out to us about her own experience, it was because she was inspired to do so by *Strange Encounter on Easter*.

[I was] inspired [to contact you] by [an] email you received [on January 10th, 2022], because it was very similar to my experience," she wrote to us via email, "here's what happened."

It was just after sunup Easter morning 1961 or 1962, a little north of Northwestern University in Illinois. I was eight or nine years old and knew there were two Easter bunnies called Mom and Dad. I have never liked mornings, but I woke up that morning just as it started to get light and decided to check out the Easter baskets for my little sister and me.

They were on the coffee table in the den, I sat on the couch and began inspecting the baskets, when I saw something unusual in our back yard. I could hardly miss it because it was in direct line of sight with the baskets, and it was big. It was a six-foot-tall, white, bipedal rabbit wearing a black vest embroidered with little glass beads of all colors (or so it seemed).

It was about 15 feet from the house, facing away from it, so I saw it in profile. It was standing still next to our seven-foot-tall blue spruce tree, about 25 to 30 feet away from me, for maybe half a minute, long enough for me to get a good look at it. It never looked in my direction; it took a short step before it hopped like a kangaroo but with shorter hops, and each hop was double the speed of the last, and the rabbit quickly became a white and black (the vest) blur and vanished before it would have hit the back fence.

After that, I poked my head into Mom and Dad's bedroom, not to see if one of them had put on the show, because I already knew that it was not a person in a rabbit costume; but if they were awake, I wanted to tell them what I saw. They were sound asleep and so was my sister, so I went back to bed and woke up at a normal time. I never uttered a sound from the time I first woke up, until the second time. Even our Airedale Terrier slept through it.

Everyone's first priority was the Easter basket opening ceremony and that's when I told my whole family what I saw, who loved it, especially my sister who was three or four years old. I have never been shy about telling folks what I saw that Easter morning from the start until this day. I'm not the Lone Ranger; I've heard other encounters with giant bunnies, be it Easter or not. It is my only anomalous experience (other than [a Near Death Experience] around age five) until decades later.

Although Sharon hadn't seen any giant animals, rabbits or otherwise, since that morning, she was reminded of the experience while watching television many years later.

"I have not seen a real giant rabbit or any other giant animal before or since, but half a century later, a related incident chilled me to the bone," she said. "It was an early scene in Steven Spielberg's miniseries Taken. When I saw the boy opening his shuttered bedroom window in the middle of the night to see a giant squirrel (?) beckoning him, my heart jumped into my throat, my knees nearly buckled, and I had shivers from head to toe. I grew up watching Svengoolie and never had that sort of reaction."

The incident caused her to question the nature of her own experience.

"Since then, I have asked myself, did I see the Easter Bunny or an [extraterrestrial] posing as the Easter Bunny? I'm going with the real Easter Bunny, because it was and still is fun, and I have never had any recollection of abduction or missing time," she said.

Sharon also kindly provided The Singular Fortean Society with an illustration of the experience that she created in Photoshop.

"It isn't photo realism, so here's an explanation of what is pictured: bottom right is the Easter basket, then our large sliding glass door to the back patio with drapes pulled back on the left and right sides, then the bunny and tree, and last is the wood fence along the side of our yard," she explained.

The experience has left an indelible mark on Sharon's memory, one that remains as crisp and clear today as it did that spring morning decades ago.

"Even after 60 years, the picture in my brain is 3D real—the grass, the needles on the blue spruce, and the snow-white fur and big, shiny, black eyes of the bunny," she said.

The memory is so powerful, in fact, that even today the idiosyncrasies of its source stick out to her.

"Note that solid white rabbits I've seen in pet stores and county fairs have pink eyes," she added.

To continue the chain of synchronicities, Sharon's report led to our third Easter Bunny sighting.

We were contacted in early 2023 by a Canadian man (name withheld by request) who wished to report his encounter with a "six-foot-tall white rabbit with a dark vest" that he had seen the Easter morning of 1988 in Crofton, British Columbia, when he was 11 years old.

According to the man, his sighting took place just before 7 a.m.

> I was looking out my bedroom window across my backyard with a backdrop of a forest. I had a rabbit cage at the border to the forest adjacent to our work shed, roughly 40 feet away. I witnessed a six-foot-tall white rabbit with a dark vest facing the door to my pet rabbit's cage.
>
> I went into shock, as I was beginning to be skeptical of such things as the Easter Bunny as I was aging out of the concept. I couldn't believe my eyes. I maintained a visual of the rabbit and pinched and slapped myself so hard to try and wake myself up. The pain confirmed I was not dreaming.
>
> I rubbed my eyes; the giant rabbit was still there.
>
> I threw open the single pane window which led to the back yard facing the rabbit cage. I yelled at the rabbit, "Hey, I see you." I tried to volley up into the window to leap out and run to the rabbit, (in my tighty white kids' underwear) but couldn't make it up out the window.
>
> It turned, looked at me, and took a series of bounds at high speed into the forest. I called my little brother, and he had arrived at the window as the giant rabbit disappeared into the Douglas firs.
>
> I woke my parents and even a neighbor. I quizzed them as to a possible Easter costume, but I knew no one could make leaps

at that speed nor have such a detailed costume, and why run for that matter. They all had a good laugh at my expense.

I explored my pet rabbit's cage and surroundings as well as the forest soon after trying to get a sense of what occurred. No tracks, no trace evidence was left behind.

The memory haunts me to this day because of the absurdity of the situation.

For some reason I thought I would google this strange experience, such as the one I had observed in my youth as it stands out in my mind to this day. Your witness's story came up in my feed and I have goose bumps as I write this. I am in disbelief and a little embarrassed but feel compelled to tell you my story because this is beyond coincidence and indicates something bigger is going on.

Currently, I am a retired police officer and forensic artist residing in Central B.C. I have witnessed strange things in my life and career, but this childhood memory was so strange, and not a hallucination. It feels like a relief to recount it, embarrassing or not. Thanks for your time.

"After the six-foot rabbit incident, I had a bizarre Mary Poppins song stuck in my head on repeat and I could not shake it. It really made no sense as I was not a fan, and it was before my time. It was odd and ill-fitting for the occurrence," he added.

In further correspondence with me, the man noted some synchronicities between his and Sharon's experiences.

"What's very strange is the woman from her 1962 encounter had the same dog as me [an Airedale Terrier] and lived in a similar type of suburb and was close to the same age and circumstance," he said.

Maybe there's something to that.

Multiple competing hypotheses exist to explain these holiday-themed encounters, with the most skeptical including dreams, hallucinations, misidentifications, and outright hoaxes, while more paranormal explanations include Santa Claus, the Easter Bunny, and other such entities existing as living thoughtforms created from human belief, along with the possibility that these images are being used as a disguise or otherwise projected by another, unrelated paranormal entity or phenomenon.

This most recent Easter Bunny encounter might favor the latter paranormal hypothesis, considering how the witness has experienced other unusual events that hint at a hidden reality surrounding us.

"Around the same time and years after [my sighting of the Easter bunny], there were instances of sleep paralysis and dreams that could be interpreted as premonitions such as family deaths and nightmares of environmental disasters," he said. "Strange occurrences...for example, the family dog would sleep at the foot of my bed, and I would find her locked outside of our house and she would be looking in my bedroom window growling at 1 a.m., or the living room couch cushions spread on the living room floor in a pattern. I would be accused of pranking by my mother in the morning. Strange noises of babies crying from the woods at night. My father would say it was cougars trying to lure prey."

The phenomena described by the man are common to many paranormal experiences, from alien abductions to ghosts and hauntings to winged humanoid and other monster sightings. While no definitive explanation yet exists for why, it is theorized by many researchers that these commonalities could represent a singular source—or at least a common background or origin—responsible for the majority of reported paranormal phenomena.

So, according to this theory, rather than these entities being the product of our minds, what we perceive them to be is an illusion projected onto our consciousnesses. What hides behind that illusion is anybody's guess.

I've long struggled with the idea that thoughtforms—such as an egregore—could be responsible for these sightings.

If you're not aware, an egregore is an occult concept that represents a non-physical being which arises out of the collective thoughts of a distinct group of people.

In other words, if enough children believe in Santa Claus, then they can bring him to life.

Sure, it works in the movies, but I haven't seen much in the way of evidence to convince me that it's definitively what is happening here.

I'm not completely ruling it out, of course. It is an intriguing concept, and I do try to be open-minded.

But I have questions.

If Santa Claus has been given life due to the power of collective belief, then why isn't he seen more often?

Millions and millions of children around the world invest their faith and hope in Santa Claus every year, and yet, all we have are a handful of mostly anonymous sighting reports. I would think that the weight of their belief might tip the scales in favor of more sightings. If all it takes to create one of these entities is for a population of people to believe in it, then we should be overrun with Santa reports.

And not just Santa.

Why aren't we seeing other examples of the same phenomenon?

That might seem rich coming from someone who just shared three Easter Bunny sighting reports but hear me out. There are a wide range of holiday figures in which folks invest significant belief, and yet, we have only a handful of reported sightings of two of them and none at all of many, many more. I expect we should have at least one Krampus sighting by now, after all.

However, in the interest of healthy debate, I do like to challenge my own position.

We don't know how many people are experiencing encounters with Santa Claus or the Easter Bunny or any other holiday icon. I think it's fair to consider that much like other potentially paranormal phenomena, what is reported represents only a fraction of what is being experienced. If that's true, then perhaps all that childlike wonder really is making the world a more magical place.

And perhaps those other holiday figures aren't popular enough to receive the amount of metaphysical fuel needed to manifest. I mean, if Santa Claus can only manage a few sightings here and there, what chance does Grýla or the Yule Cat have?

I think these are fair points and worth considering, but neither of them solves the biggest issue for me: egregores are not a proven phenomenon, and I am personally not a fan of explaining one mystery with another. Not to mention how positing the existence of a metaphysical mechanism that somehow converts belief into substance should make us wonder why people aren't just wishing better lives for themselves, which is honestly offensive in its erasure of the struggle endemic to poverty and other forms of marginalization. I mean, the jolly old elf that matches what would come out of our collective consciousness hasn't been bringing toys to any poor kids, only one witness described that, and the appearance of the figure in their report was an outlier at best. I guess all those kids not being visited by Santa must believe that they don't deserve any presents.

Now, this doesn't necessarily rule egregores out as an explanation, but it does relegate them to just one of many possibilities.

What egregores do have is the benefit of being easily the most fun.

We must consider hoaxes, of course, especially given the unknown provenance of many of the Santa sightings. But in the absence of any other evidence to support that as an explanation, it becomes simply one more possibility.

There is also mental illness or temporary hallucinations to consider, although those suffer from the same lack of supporting evidence as hoaxes.

The most skeptical among us will say that hoaxes and mental illness begin as the most credible explanations simply because they are based on phenomena we know to exist, but I find that intellectually lazy. If that's your position, then just say you're not really interested to begin with and save us all some time.

And then there are screen memories or some other manipulation of human perception.

These invasions of human consciousness are perhaps the most unsettling option available, and unfortunately, they align with many of the other reported phenomena we study.

Throughout this work—and many others, including other books I have written—you will find examples of humanity being influenced by otherworldly presences that can seemingly bend reality, or at a minimum our perception of it, to their whim.

It would seem a simple task for such an entity to appear as a beloved holiday icon—perhaps plucked from our own subconscious—for its own inscrutable reasons.

I can't shake the feeling that there is some aspect of these phenomena that is enormous and just out of sight, a depth of paranormality concealed beneath the surface of consensus reality. And it touches everything, connecting it—UFOs, ghosts, cryptids, magick, all of it.

What if that connective force just beneath the surface is consciousness itself, a universal consciousness that our brains merely act as antennae to receive, and upon which our personalities and unique consciousnesses are imprinted like waves in an ocean; individual, yet still part of the whole. Sensory organs for the universe to experience itself.

Perhaps what we're dealing with is one or more species more native than we are to this hidden reality, a being or beings with an unimaginably expansive reach, wielding power too vast for us to understand, and capable of effortless manipulation of us. Like sharks they traverse this ocean in all dimensions, utterly alien to our understanding, while we are doomed to flounder, barely able to swim.

Maybe there's something that we call faeries or ghosts or extraterrestrials but is something else entirely; something with which humanity has been interacting for a very long time that has, at different times, gone by many different names, or has at least been interpreted by us in many different ways. In this ecology of consciousness there might be a variety of inhabitants, of whom any may or may not have been misidentified to some extent throughout the ages.

The truth of this being or beings is completely unknown or, far more unsettlingly, perhaps it is unknowable. Not because it's ultimately impossible for the human mind to comprehend it, but rather, because they don't want us to know.

As Lovecraftian as that concept may seem, it is at least somewhat supported by the experiential evidence we have at present, and for that, I take it seriously.

But it is similarly unproven and far more terrifying than anything else we've considered, and for that reason, I won't judge anyone who chooses to believe that maybe, just maybe, what people are seeing really is, in some way, iconic holiday characters come to life. Perhaps, my fellow Forteans, there is a Santa Claus.

Mari Lwyd, illustration by Emily Wayland

APPENDIX A

THE MARI LWYD

The Mari Lwyd is the featured oddity in a mysterious Welsh holiday tradition wherein a horse skull is mounted on a long pole and decorated with various bright baubles and ribbons, while a person controlling it from beneath, hidden under a white cloth attached to the skull, leads a parade of characters—including such stock favorites as Punch and Judy—from door to door in search of hospitality. This strange troupe travels to people's homes between Christmas and New Year's Day, hoping to gain entrance in exchange for a song. The singers are met with much expected resistance from the residents of these homes, who respond to their song with one of their own. This exchange continues until, normally, the good-natured contest ends with the Mari Lwyd and its accompanying party being invited inside for food and drink.

The earliest known record of the Mari Lwyd comes from J. Evans' *A Tour through Part of North Wales*, in the year 1798, and at *Other Times*, published in 1800.

> A man on new year's day, dressing himself in blankets and other trappings, with a factitious head like a horse, and a party attending him, knocking for admittance, this obtained, he runs about the room with an uncommon frightful noise, which the company quit in real or pretended fright; they soon recover, and by reciting a verse of some cowydd [a form of traditional Welsh poetry], or, in default, paying a small gratuity, they gain admission.

Despite its relatively recent appearance in known texts, many in the modern pagan community have connected the tradition to pre-

Christian pagan beliefs. This connection is often tied to Rhiannon, the Welsh "Maiden of the Otherworld," who has a strong association with horses. Rhiannon is said to have ridden a white horse, faster than any other, and to have herself been forced to take the form of a horse to carry riders after having been falsely accused of her son's murder.

Believers in this connection point not only to the equine aspect of the Mari Lwyd tradition but also to the skull and its symbolic representation of death, since Rhiannon is thought to have perhaps acted as a psychopomp, given she possessed three magical birds said to wake the dead and lull the living to sleep. The Mari Lwyd, under this belief system, would then represent the cyclical acceptance and overcoming of death as the darkest days of winter give way to the eventual return of spring's fecundity. Similar associations are made with Macha, the Irish earth goddess with a strong connection to horses, and the Gallic goddess of horses, Epona, both of whom a number of scholars consider to be counterparts to Rhiannon.

Late 19th and early 20th century folklorists David Jones and Iorwerth C. Peate translated the Mari Lwyd as "Blessed Mary" or "Holy Mary," respectively, arguing that there is a Christian connection to the tradition. To Peate, that connection was a pagan ceremony that had been renamed after the Virgin Mary in the Middle Ages. But Jones took the association with Christianity even further, suggesting that the entire tradition arose out of the Feast of the Ass, a festival commemorating the flight of Mary and Joseph into Egypt, historically marked on January 14th. In this interpretation, the Mari Lwyd represents the donkey on which Mary rode.

These explanations have since fallen out of favor due to a lack of evidence to support the tradition existing in antiquity. A more popular modern hypothesis is that the Mari Lwyd arose out of a "hooded animal" tradition which exists throughout Britain in various forms; a tradition identified by 20th century folklorist E.C. Cawte, who translated the Mari Lwyd as "Grey Mare." Features noted by Cawte to be common to these customs were the use of a hobby horse, the performance at Christmas time, a song or spoken statement requesting payment, and the use of a team which includes a man dressed in women's clothing. This approach aims at objectivity, neither accepting nor denying any unproven connections to religious belief systems, but rather admitting that the origin is a mystery— one that may or may not have been influenced by preexisting beliefs.

Despite a dip in popularity in the early 1900s, by mid-century the tradition of the Mari Lwyd had been resurrected and is still popularly practiced throughout Wales today. So, if a terrifying horse skull wearing a white sheet turns up at your door accompanied by a troupe of strange characters this Yuletide season, feel free to invite them in for some holiday cheer, but not before engaging them in a glorious sing-off—just make sure to put up a good fight, that's half the fun.

Inspired by Victorian Christmas Ghost Stories, illustration by Emily Wayland

Appendix B

Victorian Christmas Ghost Stories

Ghost stories told at Christmas arose out of the same winter traditions that gave us many of our frightful holiday monsters. The darkest time of year has long been associated with ghosts, dating back at least to the celebration of Yule—a time when the unquiet dead were thought to be particularly active. Stuck inside during the frigid darkness of winter, people often entertained themselves with stories to match the spookiness of their environment. Even after Christianity supplanted Anglo Saxon paganism in England, the tradition of telling supernatural tales continued.

This tradition took on new life in the Victorian era. With more people moving into the cities, an expanding middle class, and the ability of the steam powered printing press to quickly reproduce literature, there was a thriving market for the kinds of spooky stories that so many folks had grown up hearing. A market that writers of the time were more than happy to fill.

Most readers are familiar with the popular 1843 Christmas ghost story *A Christmas Carol*, and with good reason: its author, Charles Dickens, played a huge part in popularizing the genre. In addition to writing his seminal holiday classic, Dickens also wrote several other ghostly Christmas novellas, in addition to editing even more such stories from other authors and working them into magazines he was editing.

But it could be that these are more than just stories.

Researcher Amanda Woomer wrote in her work, *A Very Frightful Victorian Christmas*, "Many times, people have paranormal encounters with deceased friends and family during the winter months. Even throughout the Victorian age, many of the stories shared on Christmas Eve were actual ghostly encounters people experienced and not just fictional fantasies. It would seem grief, like ghost stories, transcends time."

While we can't say the following story is based on any factual experience, it is an excellent example of the kinds of stories that circulated in Victorian England around Christmas.

Presented here for your perusal is *The Kit-Bag* by Algernon Blackwood, first published for *Pall Mall Magazine* in December 1908.

THE KIT BAG
by Algernon Blackwood

When the words "Not Guilty" sounded through the crowded courtroom that dark December afternoon, Arthur Wilbraham, the great criminal KC, and leader for the triumphant defence, was represented by his junior; but Johnson, his private secretary, carried the verdict across to his chambers like lightning.

"It's what we expected, I think," said the barrister, without emotion; "and, personally, I am glad the case is over." There was no particular sign of pleasure that his defence of John Turk, the murderer, on a plea of insanity, had been successful, for no doubt he felt, as everybody who had watched the case felt, that no man had ever better deserved the gallows.

"I'm glad too," said Johnson. He had sat in the court for ten days watching the face of the man who had carried out with callous detail one of the most brutal and cold-blooded murders of recent years.

The counsel glanced up at his secretary. They were more than employer and employed; for family and other reasons, they were friends. "Ah, I remember; yes," he said with a kind smile, "and you want to get away for Christmas? You're going to skate and ski in the Alps, aren't you? If I was your age I'd come with you."

Johnson laughed shortly. He was a young man of twenty-six, with a delicate face like a girl's. "I can catch the morning boat now," he said; "but that's not the reason I'm glad the trial is over. I'm glad it's over because I've seen the last of that man's dreadful face. It positively haunted me. Bat white skin, with the black hair brushed low over the forehead, is a thing I shall never forget, and the description of the way the dismembered body was crammed and packed with lime into that—"

"Don't dwell on it, my dear fellow," interrupted the other, looking at him curiously out of his keen eyes, "don't think about it. Such pictures have a trick of coming back when one least wants them." He paused a moment. "Now go," he added presently, "and enjoy your holiday. I shall want all your energy for my Parliamentary work when you get back. And don't break your neck skiing."

Johnson shook hands and took his leave. At the door he turned suddenly.

"I knew there was something I wanted to ask you," he said. "Would you mind lendang me one of your kit-bags? It's too late to get one tonight, and I leave in the morning before the shops are open."

"Of course; I'll send Henry over with it to your rooms. You shall have it the moment I get home."

"I promise to take great care of it," said Johnson gratefully, delighted to think that within thirty hours he would be nearing the brilliant sunshine of the high Alps in winter. The thought of that criminal court was like an evil dream in his mind.

He dined at his club and went on to Bloomsbury, where he occupied the top floor in one of those old, gaunt houses in which the rooms are large and lofty. The floor below his own was vacant and unfurnished, and below that were other lodgers whom he did not know. It was cheerless, and he looked forward heartily to a change. The night was even more cheerless: it was miserable, and few people were about. A cold, sleety rain was driving down the streets before the keenest east wind he had ever felt. It howled dismally among the big, gloomy houses of the great squares, and when he reached his rooms he heard it whistling and shouting over the world of black roofs beyond his windows.

In the hall he met his landlady, shading a candle from the draughts with her thin hand. "This come by a man from Mr. Wilbr'im's, sir."

She pointed to what was evidently the kit-bag, and Johnson

thanked her and took it upstairs with him. "I shall be going abroad in the morning for ten days, Mrs Monks," he said. "I'll leave an address for letters."

"And I hope you'll 'ave a merry Christmas, sir," she said, in a raucous, wheezy voice that suggested spirits, "and better weather than this."

"I hope so too," replied her lodger, shuddering a little as the wind went roaring down the street outside.

When he got upstairs he heard the sleet volleying against the window panes. He put his kettle on to make a cup of hot coffee, and then set about putting a few things in order for his absence. "And now I must pack—such as my packing is," he laughed to himself, and set to work at once.

He liked the packing, for it brought the snow mountains so vividly before him, and made him forget the unpleasant scenes of the past ten days. Besides, it was not elaborate in nature. His friend had lent him thevery thing—a stout canvas kit-bag, sack-shaped, with holes round the neck for the brass bar and padlock. It was a bit shapeless, true, and not much to look at, but its capacity was unlimited, and there was no need to pack carefully. He shoved in his waterproof coat, his fur cap and gloves, his skates and climbing boots, his sweaters, snow-boots, and ear-caps; and then on the top of these he piled his woollen shirts and underwear, his thick socks, puttees, and knickerbockers. The dress suit came next, in case the hotel people dressed for dinner, and then, thinking of the best way to pack his white shirts, he paused a moment to reflect. "That's the worst of these kit-bags," he mused vaguely, standing in the centre of the sitting-room, where he had come to fetch some string.

It was after ten o'clock. A furious gust of wind rattled the windows as though to hurry him up, and he thought with pity of the poor Londoners whose Christmas would be spent in such a climate, whilst he was skimming over snowy slopes in bright sunshine, and dancing in the evening with rosy-cheeked girls—Ah! that reminded him; he must put in his dancing-pumps and evening socks. He crossed over from his sitting-room to the cupboard on the landing where he kept his linen.

And as he did so he heard someone coming softly up the stairs.

He stood still a moment on the landing to listen. It was Mrs Monks's step, he thought; she must he coming up with the last post. But then the steps ceased suddenly, and he heard no more. They were at least two flights down, and he came to the conclusion they were too heavy to be those of his bibulous landlady. No doubt they belonged to a late lodger who had mistaken his floor. He went into his bedroom and packed his pumps and dress-shirts as best he could.

The kit-bag by this time was two-thirds full, and stood upright on its own base like a sack of flour. For the first time he noticed that it was old and dirty, the canvas faded and worn, and that it had obviously been subjected to rather rough treatment. It was not a very nice bag to have sent him—certainly not a new one, or one that his chief valued. He gave the matter a passing thought, and went on with his packing. Once or twice, however, he caught himself wondering who it could have been wandering down below, for Mrs Monks had not come up with letters, and the floor was empty and unfurnished. From time to time, moreover, he was almost certain he heard a soft tread of someone padding about over the bare boards--cautiously, stealthily, as silently as possible—and, further, that the sounds had been lately coming distinctly nearer.

For the first time in his life he began to feel a little creepy. Then, as though to emphasize this feeling, an odd thing happened: as he left the bedroom, having, just packed his recalcitrant white shirts, he noticed that the top of the kit-bag lopped over towards him with an extraordinary resemblance to a human face. The canvas fell into a fold like a nose and forehead, and the brass rings for the padlock just filled the position of the eyes. A shadow—or was it a travel stain? for he could not tell exactly— looked like hair. It gave him rather a turn, for it was so absurdly, so outrageously, like the face of John Turk the murderer.

He laughed, and went into the front room, where the light was stronger.

"That horrid case has got on my mind," he thought; "I shall be glad of achange of scene and air." In the sitting-room, however, he was not pleased to hear again that stealthy tread upon the stairs, and to realize that it was much closer than before, as well as unmistakably real. And this time he got up and went out to see who it could be creeping about on the upper staircase at so late an hour.

But the sound ceased; there was no one visible on the stairs. He went to the floor below, not without trepidation, and turned on the electric light to make sure that no one was hiding in the empty rooms of the unoccupied suite. There was not a stick of furniture large enough to hide a dog. Then he called over the banisters to Mrs Monks, but there was no answer, and his voice echoed down into the dark vault of the house, and was lost in the roar of the gale that howled outside. Everyone was in bed and asleep—everyone except himself and the owner of this soft and stealthy tread.

"My absurd imagination, I suppose," he thought. "It must have been thewind after all, although—it seemed so very real and close, I thought."He went back to his packing. It was by this time getting on towards midnight. He drank his coffee up and lit another pipe—the last beforeturning in.

It is difficult to say exactly at what point fear begins, when the causesof that fear are not plainly before the eyes. Impressions gather on the surface of the mind, film by film, as ice gathers upon the surface of still water, but often so lightly that they claim no definite recognition from the consciousness. Then a point is reached where the accumulated impressions become a definite emotion, and the mind realizes that something has happened. With something of a start, Johnson suddenly recognized that he felt nervous—oddly nervous; also, that for some time past the causes of this feeling had been gathering slowly in has mind, but that he had only just reached the point where he was forced to acknowledge them.
It was a singular and curious malaise that had come over him, and he hardly knew what to make of it. He felt as though he were doing something that was strongly objected to by another person, another person, moreover, who had some right to object. It was a most disturbing and disagreeable feeling, not unlike the persistent promptings of conscience: almost, in fact, as if he were doing something he knew to be wrong. Yet, though he searched vigorously and honestly in his mind, he could nowhere lay his finger upon the secret of this growing uneasiness, and it perplexed him. More, it distressed and frightened him.

"Pure nerves, I suppose," he said aloud with a forced laugh. "Mountain air will cure all that! Ah," he added, still speaking to himself, "and that reminds me—my snow-glasses."

He was standing by the door of the bedroom during this brief soliloquy, and as he passed quickly towards the sitting-room to fetch them from the cupboard he saw out of the corner of his eye the indistinct outline of a figure standing on the stairs, a few feet from the top. It was someone in a stooping position, with one hand on the banisters, and the face peering up towards the landing. And at the same moment he heard a shuffling footstep. The person who had been creeping about below all this time had at last come up to his own floor. Who in the world could it be? And what in the name of Heaven did he want?

Johnson caught his breath sharply and stood stock still. Then, after a few seconds' hesitation, he found his courage, and turned to investigate.

The stairs, he saw to his utter amazement, were empty; there was no one.

He felt a series of cold shivers run over him, and something about the muscles of his legs gave a little and grew weak. For the space of several minutes he peered steadily into the shadows that congregated about the top of the staircase where he had seen the figure, and then he walked fast—almost ran, in fact—into the light of the front room; but hardly had he passed inside the doorway when he heard someone come up the stairs behind him with a quick bound and go swiftly into his bedroom. It was a heavy, but at the same time a stealthy footstep—the tread of somebody who did not wish to be seen. And it was at this precise moment that the nervousness he had hitherto experienced leaped the boundary line, and entered the state of fear, almost of acute, unreasoning fear. Before it turned into terror there was a further boundary to cross, and beyond that again lay the region of pure horror. Johnson's position was an unenviable one.

"By Jove! That was someone on the stairs, then," he muttered, his flesh crawling all over; "and whoever it was has now gone into my bedroom." His delicate, pale face turned absolutely white, and for some minutes he hardly knew what to think or do. Then he realized intuitively that delay only set a premium upon fear; and he crossed the landing boldly and went straight into the other room, where, a few seconds before, the steps had disappeared.

"Who's there? Is that you, Mrs. Monks?" he called aloud, as he went, and heard the first half of his words echo down the empty stairs, while the second half fell dead against the curtains in a room that apparently held no other human figure than his own.

"Who's there?" he called again, in a voice unnecessarily loud and that only just held firm. "What do you want here?"

The curtains swayed very slightly, and, as he saw it, his heart felt as if it almost missed a beat; yet he dashed forward and drew them aside with a rush. A window, streaming with rain, was all that met his gaze. He continued his search, but in vain; the cupboards held nothing but rows of clothes, hanging motionless; and under the bed there was no sign of anyone hiding. He stepped backwards into the middle of the room, and, as he did so, something all but tripped him up. Turning with a sudden spring of alarm he saw—the kit-bag.

he did so, something all but tripped him up. Turning with a sudden spring of alarm he saw—the kit-bag.

"Odd!" he thought. "That's not where I left it!" A few moments before it had surely been on his right, between the bed and the bath; he did not remember having moved it. It was very curious. What in the world was the matter with everything? Were all his senses gone queer? A terrific gust of wind tore at the windows, dashing the sleet against the glass with the force of small gunshot, and then fled away howling dismally over the waste of Bloomsbury roofs. A sudden vision of the Channel next day rose in his mind and recalled him sharply to realities.

"There's no one here at any rate; that's quite clear!" he exclaimed aloud. Yet at the time he uttered them he knew perfectly well that his words were not true and that he did not believe them himself. He felt exactly as though someone was hiding close about him, watching all his movements, trying to hinder his packing in some way. "And two of my senses," he added, keeping up the pretense, "have played me the most absurd tricks: the steps I heard and the figure I saw were both entirely imaginary."

He went hack to the front room, poked the fire into a blaze, and sat down before it to think. What impressed him more than anything else was the fact that the kit-bag was no longer where he had left it. It had been dragged nearer to the door.

What happened afterwards that night happened, of course, to a man already excited by fear, and was perceived by a mind that had not the full and proper control, therefore, of the senses. Outwardly, Johnson remained calm and master of himself to the end, pretending to the very last that everything he witnessed had a natural explanation, or was merely delusions of his tired nerves. But inwardly, in his very heart, he knew all along that someone had been hiding downstairs in the empty suite when he came in, that this person had watched his opportunity and then stealthily made his way up to the bedroom, and that all he saw and heard afterwards, from the moving of the kit-bag to—well, to the other things this story has to tell—were caused directly by the presence of this invisible person.

And it was here, just when he most desired to keep his mind and thoughts controlled, that the vivid pictures received day after day upon the mental plates exposed in the courtroom of the Old Bailey, came strongly to light and developed themselves in the dark room of his inner vision. Unpleasant, haunting memories have a way of coming to life again just when the mind least desires them—in the silent watches of the night, on sleepless pillows, during the lonely hours spent by sick and dying beds.

And so now, in the same way, Johnson saw nothing but the dreadful face of John Turk, the murderer, lowering at him from every corner of his mental field of vision; the white skin, the evil eyes, and the fringe of black hair low over the forehead. All the pictures of those ten days in court crowded back into his mind unbidden, and very vivid.

"This is all rubbish and nerves," he exclaimed at length, springing with sudden energy from his chair. "I shall finish my packing and go to bed. I'm overwrought, overtired. No doubt, at this rate I shall hear steps and things all night!"

But his face was deadly white all the same. He snatched up his field-glasses and walked across to the bedroom, humming a music-hall song as he went—a trifle too loud to be natural; and the instant he crossed the threshold and stood within the room something turned cold about his heart, and he felt that every hair on his head stood up.

The kit-bag lay close in front of him, several feet nearer to the door than he had left it, and just over its crumpled top he saw a head and face slowly sinking down out of sight as though someone were crouching behind it to hide, and at the same moment a sound like a long-drawn sigh was distinctly audible in the still air about him between the gusts of the storm outside.

Johnson had more courage and will-power than the girlish indecision of his face indicated; but at first such a wave of terror came over him that for some seconds he could do nothing but stand and stare. A violent trembling ran down his back and legs, and he was conscious of a foolish, almost a hysterical, impulse to scream aloud. That sigh seemed in his very ear, and the air still quivered with it. It was unmistakably a human sigh.

"Who's there?" he said at length, finding his voice; but though he meant to speak with loud decision, the tones came out instead in a faint whisper, for he had partly lost the control of his tongue and lips.

He stepped forward, so that he could see all round and over the kit-bag. Of course there was nothing there, nothing but the faded carpet and the bulgang canvas sides. He put out his hands and threw open the mouth of the sack where it had fallen over, being only three parts full, and then he saw for the first time that round the inside, some six inches from the top, there ran a broad smear of dull crimson. It was an old and faded blood stain. He uttered a scream, and drew back his hands as if they had been burnt. At the same moment the kit-bag gave a faint, but unmistakable, lurch forward towards the door.

Johnson collapsed backwards, searching with his hands for the support of something solid, and the door, being further behind him than he realized, received his weight just in time to prevent his falling, and shut to with a resounding bang. At the same moment the swinging of his left arm accidentally touched the electric switch, and the light in the room went out.

It was an awkward and disagreeable predicament, and if Johnson had not been possessed of real pluck he might have done all manner of foolish things. As it was, however, he pulled himself together, and groped furiously for the little brass knob to turn the light on again. But the rapid closing of the door had set the coats hanging on it a-swinging, and his fingers became entangled in a confusion of sleeves and pockets, so that it was some moments before he found the switch. And in those few moments of bewilderment and terror two things happened that sent him beyond recall over the boundary into the region of genuine horror—he distinctly heard the kit-bag shuffling heavily across the floor in jerks, and close in front of his face sounded once again the sigh of a human being.

In his anguished efforts to find the brass button on the wall he nearly scraped the nails from his fingers, but even then, in those frenzied moments of alarm—so swift and alert are the impressions of a mind keyed-up by a vivid emotion—he had time to realize that he dreaded the return of the light, and that it might be better for him to stay hidden in the merciful screen of darkness. It was but the impulse of a moment, however, and before he had time to act upon it he had yielded automatically to the original desire, and the room was flooded again with light.

But the second instinct had been right. It would have been better for him to have stayed in the shelter of the kind darkness. For there, close before him, bending over the half-packed kit-bag, clear as life in the merciless glare of the electric light, stood the figure of John Turk, the murderer. Not three feet from him the man stood, the fringe of black hair marked plainly against the pallor of the forehead, the whole horrible presentment of the scoundrel, as vivid as he had seen him day after day in the Old Bailey, when he stood there in the dock, cynical and callous, under the very shadow of the gallows.

In a flash Johnson realized what it all meant: the dirty and much-used bag; the smear of crimson within the top; the dreadful stretched condition of the bulging sides. He remembered how the victim's body had been stuffed into a canvas bag for burial, the ghastly, dismembered fragments forced with lime into this very bag; and the bag itself produced as evidence—it all came back to him as clear as day...

Very softly and stealthily his hand groped behind him for the handle of the door, but before he could actually turn it the very thing that he most of all dreaded came about, and John Turk lifted his devil's face and looked at him. At the same moment that heavy sigh passed through the air of the room, formulated somehow into words: "It's my bag. And I want it."

Johnson just remembered clawing the door open, and then falling in a heap upon the floor of the landing, as he tried frantically to make his way into the front room.

He remained unconscious for a long time, and it was still dark when he opened his eyes and realized that he was lying, stiff and bruised, on the cold boards. Then the memory of what he had seen rushed back into his mind, and he promptly fainted again. When he woke the second time the wintry dawn was just beginning to peep in at the windows, painting the stairs a cheerless, dismal grey, and he managed to crawl into the front room, and cover himself with an overcoat in the armchair, where at length he fell asleep.

A great clamour woke him. He recognized Mrs. Monks's voice, loud and voluble.

"What! You ain't been to bed, sir! Are you ill, or has anything 'appened? And there's an urgent gentleman to see you, though it ain't seven o'clock yet, and—"

"Who is it?" he stammered. "I'm all right, thanks. Fell asleep in my chair, I suppose."

"Someone from Mr. Wilb'rim's, and he says he ought to see you quick before you go abroad, and I told him—"

"Show him up, please, at once," said Johnson, whose head was whirling, and his mind was still full of dreadful visions.

Mr. Wilbraham's man came in with many apologies, and explained briefly and quickly that an absurd mistake had been made, and that the wrong kit-bag had been sent over the night before.

"Henry somehow got hold of the one that came over from the courtroom, and Mr. Wilbraham only discovered it when he saw his own lying in his room, and asked why it had not gone to you," the man said.

"Oh!" said Johnson stupidly.

"And he must have brought you the one from the murder case instead, sir, I'm afraid," the man continued, without the ghost of an expression on his face. "The one John Turk packed the dead both in. Mr. Wilbraham's awful upset about it, sir, and told me to come over first thing this morning with the right one, as you were leaving by the boat."

He pointed to a clean-looking kit-bag on the floor, which he had just brought. "And I was to bring the other one back, sir," he added casually.

For some minutes Johnson could not find his voice. At last he pointed in the direction of his bedroom. "Perhaps you would kindly unpack it for me. Just empty the things out on the floor."

The man disappeared into the other room, and was gone for five minutes. Johnson heard the shifting to and fro of the bag, and the rattle of the skates and boots being unpacked.

"Thank you, sir," the man said, returning with the bag folded over his arm. "And can I do anything more to help you, sir?"

"What is it?" asked Johnson, seeing that he still had something he wished to say.

The man shuffled and looked mysterious. "Beg pardon, sir, but knowing your interest in the Turk case, I thought you'd maybe like to know what's happened —"

"Yes."

"John Turk killed hisself last night with poison immediately on getting his release, and he left a note for Mr. Wilbraham saying as he'd be much obliged if they'd have him put away, same as the woman he murdered, in the old kit-bag."

"What time — did he do it?" asked Johnson.

"Ten o'clock last night, sir, the warder says."

The End

TOBIAS WAYLAND

AUTHOR

Tobias Wayland is a passionate Fortean who has been actively investigating the unusual for over a decade. The first several years of his investigative career were spent as a MUFON field investigator and following that he investigated independently prior to becoming the head writer and editor for The Singular Fortean Society. Tobias is a frequent guest on various podcasts and radio shows, has written several books and contributed articles to periodicals on the paranormal, has appeared on television and in documentaries, and is often invited to speak at paranormal conferences and events.

He was featured in the series premiere of *Expedition X*, and the Small Town Monsters documentaries *Terror in the Skies* and *On the Trail of the Lake Michigan Mothman* for his work investigating Mothman sightings around Lake Michigan. He and his wife Emily have been involved with the Lake Michigan Mothman investigation since its advent in the spring of 2017, and published a book chronicling the experience, *The Lake Michigan Mothman: High Strangeness in the Midwest*. His second and third books about unusual phenomena, *Strange Tales of the Impossible* and *The Singular Fortean Society's Yuletide Guide to High Strangeness*, continue their work in investigating a variety of seemingly impossible events.

His years as an investigator have served him best by illustrating that when it comes to the anomalous, the preternatural, and the paranormal, any answers he's found are still hopelessly outnumbered by questions.

EMILY WAYLAND

ILLUSTRATOR

Emily Wayland is an ardent craftsperson and devoted monster enthusiast. An accomplished artist, designer, and photographer, Emily is responsible not only for The Singular Fortean Society's aesthetic, but also the examination of any photographic or video evidence. Emily's art and designs have been featured in various paranormal art shows around the Minneapolis area, and on television and documentaries featuring the work of The Singular Fortean Society. In addition, she has designed all the covers for *The Feminine Macabre* anthology series, as well as contributing an essay for its second volume. Her expertise is also sought after as a speaker and guest at conferences and on podcasts.

She and her husband Tobias have been involved with the Lake Michigan Mothman investigation since its advent in the spring of 2017, and published a book chronicling the experience, *The Lake Michigan Mothman: High Strangeness in the Midwest*. She is also featured in the Small Town Monsters documentary *On the Trail of the Lake Michigan Mothman* for her part in investigating the mystery.

Her lifetime love affair with monsters of all varieties has led her to pursue them in real life, and she hopes that her expertise in photography will help her capture one—at least on film.

JOSHUA CUTCHIN

Joshua Cutchin is a full-time author and musician specializing in speculative non-fiction. He is the author of seven critically-acclaimed books. Joshua's most recent non-fiction publication is the two-part 2022 entry entitled *Ecology of Souls: A New Mythology of Death & the Paranormal*, which seeks to reconcile ancient concepts of the soul with modern phenomena such as UFOs, fairy sightings, cryptid encounters, and extended consciousness. He has headlined as a guest speaker at numerous paranormal conventions throughout the United States, has appeared on hundreds of podcasts, and in 2019 was featured on the hit History Channel series *Ancient Aliens*. 2023 saw the release of his first work of fiction, the novel *Them Old Ways Never Died*.

OTHER TITLES from
THE SINGULAR FORTEAN SOCIETY

THE LAKE MICHIGAN MOTHMAN
HIGH STRANGENESS IN THE MIDWEST

This book represents over two years of research by a dedicated team of investigators who have taken dozens of reports of a weird, winged humanoid seen around Lake Michigan. Author and investigator Tobias Wayland has collected these reports for the first time in one volume, along with his analysis and insider perspective as a member of the investigative team. The phenomena described within represent the continuation of a decades-long series of events first recorded in Point Pleasant, West Virginia, in the late '60s, but that has likely been with humanity since our advent, and seems just as likely to be with us until our end.

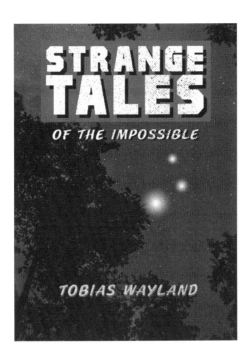

Made in the USA
Columbia, SC
11 December 2023

28278649R00102